7 Principles to Live a Champion Life

John Di Lemme

7 Principles to Live a Champion Life
Copyright © 2008 John Di Lemme

Di Lemme Development Group, Inc.
931 Village Boulevard
Suite 905-366
West Palm Beach, Florida 33409-1939
(561) 847-3467
www.LifestyleFreedomClub.com

All rights reserved. No part of this book may be used or reproduced by any means, graphics, electronic, or mechanical, including photocopying, recording, taping or by any information storage retrieval system without the written permission of the author, John Di Lemme. Please contact Team@LifestyleFreedomClub.com to request permission to use quotes from this material.

This book is designed to provide competent and reliable information regarding the subject matters covered. However, it is sold with the understanding that the author is not engaged in rendering legal, financial, or other professional advice. Laws and practices often vary from state to state and if legal or other expert assistance is required, the services of a professional should be sought. The author specifically disclaims any liability that is incurred from the use and/or application of the contents of this book.

ISBN: 978-1-257-04385-9

Dedication

This book is dedicated to all of the Champions out there that struggle to succeed yet refuse to give up. Remember, you are born a Champion and your certificate of life gives you the right to achieve everything that your heart desires. You are a Champion!

Table of Contents

Foreword by Gold Medalist Nikki Stone

Principle I: Learn the True Meaning of Freedom

Principle II: Know Who You Are

Principle III: Understand Feelings versus Emotions

Principle IV: Answer Life-Changing Questions

Principle V: Insure Your Dream

Principle VI: Make a Decision not an Excuse

Principle VII: Success is in Your Seed

Foreword

A champion is defined as a winner, victor, defender, advocate and protector. These powerful words fully describe the kind of speaker, mentor, and coach that John Di Lemme is to thousands worldwide. In this book, John has unselfishly shared the strategies and secrets to truly living a champion life. His ability to divulge this wisdom came from years of building his own life and career on a strong foundation of integrity and his commitment to changing lives around the globe. As an Olympian, I fully understand the hard work and determination it takes to achieve your goals in life, and I admire John Di Lemme's no holds barred approach to fulfill his ultimate destiny. I have absolutely no doubt that this book will radically improve your level of success and change your life forever.

Nikki Stone, Olympic Gold Medalist & Best Selling Author of *"When Turtles Fly"*

Principle I
Learn True Meaning of Freedom

Freedom is a very powerful word. Webster's dictionary defines freedom in many different ways, but this is the one that really stuck out to me. Freedom is the state of being free - liberated from slavery, restraint or the power of another. When I read this definition, the Bible verse Acts 12:7 ran through my mind - *And, behold, the angel of the Lord came upon him, and a light shined in the prison: and he smote Peter on the side, and raised him up, saying, Arise up quickly. And his chains fell off from his hands.* Can you imagine the delight in Peter's heart as those chains released his hands and he was no longer in captivity?

You too have the opportunity to escape captivity and live in freedom for the rest of your life. Can you imagine actually being free financially, spiritually, socially, emotionally and physically? For most people that seems completely unrealistic, but I'm here to tell you it can be your reality. Remember, inside the word impossible is possible. It is possible for you to have freedom in every area of your life!

In the United States, we observe Independence Day on the fourth of July. There are fireworks exploding in the air across America in celebration of our freedom, which was made possible by the signing of the Declaration of Independence in 1776. When that document was signed, it was "declared" that America was free. Let me ask you a question. When will you declare your independence? When will you declare your freedom? Before you can achieve it, you must believe it so say it out loud now...I DECLARE THAT I AM FREE IN EVERY AREA OF MY LIFE! THE SHACKLES ARE GONE! I AM FREE!

After you declare that you are free, you need to understand exactly what freedom is to you. If you don't know what it is, then how are you going to achieve it? What is freedom to you? I'm going to break down each letter of the word F-R-E-E-D-O-M, and I want you to visualize what it really means to you.

The first letter in the word freedom is 'F', which stands for focus. Are you focused on being free in every area of your life? If not, then you need to shift your focus and become focused on your freedom. Most people don't become truly free in their lives, because they are comfortable or simply aren't courageous enough to stretch themselves beyond their current life boundaries. Take advantage of getting uncomfortable and stretching yourself, because to be free you have to do things differently than most people.

Just imagine standing inside of an average size circle every single day. Your current job, friends, habits and overall way of life are also in the circle. Can you feel it getting tight? Don't you have the urge to step outside the circle? Now, imagine extending your foot, stepping outside of the circle and feeling an ultimate sense of relief. You have room to move and make decisions that you couldn't make inside that circle. Sadly, you will never get to leave that circle because it's the limit that you've placed on your life unless you make the decision get focused on your freedom and stretch yourself outside of your comfort zone.

Whatever you focus on every day will determine whether or not you achieve freedom in your life. One of the main objectives that you should focus on is taking advantage of every single minute in your day. If you are scheduled and plan your day, then you are forging forward towards freedom. On the other hand, if you lay in bed at night, reflect back on your day and have no idea what you did all day long, then you are allowing time to take advantage of you. I often hear people say, "I have no idea where the time went." It's one of those moments when I have to bite my tongue, because I want to tell that person that they are wasting their time instead of investing it.

Time is our biggest form of currency so we must spend it wisely. If you focus on freedom and invest your time wisely, then you are one day closer to being free instead of remaining entrapped. While working with one of my coaching students, I asked her to show me her planner. I wanted to know where she was investing her time, because she was stuck in a rut. Surprisingly, she had every single minute of her day scheduled. This woman knew where she was every minute of the day and led an extremely busy lifestyle. However, I looked closer at the actual activity and saw the issue. I explained to her that just because she was active didn't mean that she was productive. She filled her day with meaningless tasks that created activity instead of accomplishment. Just because your calendar is full doesn't mean that you are investing your time wisely. I encourage you to sit down and take a good look at where you're spending your time and how some of those insignificant, waste of time activities are pushing you further away from your freedom.

Another determining factor in whether or not you become free is what you actually look at on a daily basis. I love to take photos with other champions at events and have built a Why wall in my office in South Florida. This wall is filled with not only pictures but also letters, art, cards and many more positive, inspirational things that I have received from people all over the world. In my home office or as I prefer to call it my "construction zone", I have pictures of my own dreams and goals. I focus on these things every day as I sit in my construction zone and build my business. No matter the obstacle that I encounter, I'm constantly reminded of my Why in life, because I see it in front of me.

What are you looking at? If your answer to that question is "nothing", then that's exactly what you are doing to achieve freedom in your life…NOTHING. In my favorite book, The Bible, it states that a man without a vision will perish. Another way of saying it is that a person without focus in pursuit of his dream will fail. I cringe when see someone reading those garbage books and magazines that highlight all the gloom and doom in the world. Can you really expect to achieve freedom in your life if you are focusing your mind and eyes on that trash? I challenge you to throw out the garbage and start reading positive, inspirational material. You can also take it a step further and hang some pictures of your dreams and goals in your construction zone. You won't believe how quickly your results will skyrocket when your focus is shifted!

If you're saying, "That sounds easy. All I have to do is organize my planner and hang a few pictures then I will be focused on achieving freedom in my life." YOU ARE WRONG! It's not a one step process. It's daily focus in every area of your life. When I say that you have to be focused, I don't mean that you just simply think about freedom sometime during the day. You need to be focused like a sniper with a laser pointed at his target...laser-focused! If you let anything or anyone distract you, then your target (freedom) will no longer be in sight.

The next letter in the word freedom is 'R', which stands for regret. Let me give you an illustration. Imagine an elderly man sitting in his rocking chair looking back over his life. He has many good memories, but the regret that he has for not taking chances and stepping out in faith overshadows those memories. He wishes that he would have been more focused on his dreams for himself and his family rather than simply living paycheck to paycheck and longing for Friday. He knows that he missed out on so many things in life, because he didn't have the courage to follow his heart instead of his mind. Now, I know that nobody wants to spend the last years of their life in regret but so many people end up in that place.

You have to understand regret as it pertains to your life now. Here's a harsh reality for many people...If you don't challenge yourself to get focused on your freedom, then you will be sitting in that same rocking chair pondering where things went wrong and regretting your decisions. When you change the way that you view life, stretch yourself outside of your comfort zone and become laser-focused on your freedom, regret diminishes. One of my favorite Jim Rohn quotes says it all - *We must all suffer from one of two pains: the pain of discipline or the pain of regret. The difference is discipline weighs ounces while regret weighs tons.* If you don't discipline yourself to change, then you are destined to be consumed with regret later on in life.

I see people all over the world that challenge themselves to change. They are stepping out in faith and focusing on their goals and dreams but then it happens. They encounter adversity, give up and go back to their old, comfortable ways. For most of us, our road to success is not paved in gold. As you're walking along and forging forward, you will encounter road blocks that cause doubt and fear in your mind as to whether you can really make it. So, what do you do? I know the next letter in the word freedom is 'E', but I need to give you another word for 'R' to answer that question.

'R' also stands for return. When FEAR gets in the way, there are four things that you must do - Face it, Extinguish it, Attack it and Return. When you face that fear, you stand in the presence of the enemy and let him know that nothing will stop you from achieving freedom. Extinguish and attack that fear by declaring that you are free. Scream it out loud...I DECLARE I AM FREE! FEAR GET OUT OF MY WAY! The final step is to return to proceeding forward down your success path. It's your way of letting everyone know...I'M BACK AND NOTHING IS GOING TO STOP ME!

Many times, the fear that gets in the way of you achieving your freedom is brought on by other people. When you are surrounded by people that constantly bring you down or tell you that you are going nowhere in life, you have to make the decision to leave those people behind. I know that sounds harsh, but after you have achieved your freedom you will be able to return to those same people and show them a better way.

When I was eighteen years old, I was diagnosed as a stutterer. It was official. I would never be able to speak fluently. Deep in my heart, I knew that I could speak. I made the decision to leave those doctors and other people behind that labeled me as a stutterer. It wasn't easy to leave some of my friends, but I knew that I simply couldn't listen to them anymore. Since then, I have returned to many of them and explained how my focus and determination led to my new label – International Motivational Speaker. I made the decision in my life to accept the pain of change and discipline rather than live with the pain of regret forever.

The next letter in freedom is 'E', which stands for enjoy. Enjoy your success journey and envision it as a rollercoaster with many twists and turns. Sometimes it may even flip upside down and scare the living daylights out of you, but you know when you step off the ride at the end you will see only one thing…FREEDOM. Enjoy the journey. Enjoy the challenge. Enjoy the twists, turns and ups and downs and look forward to enjoying the success that you have achieved at the end of the ride.

There are actually rollercoaster clubs that come together from all over the world to ride the greatest rollercoasters ever built. These enthusiasts enjoy not only the amazing rides but also the friendships that are developed through their hobby. Think about it. You stand in line for the ride, and the anticipation builds. You climb into the seat, and you start moving forward. You hear the clicking of the tracks as it takes you to the top of the big loop. As you get ready to plunge into a downward spiral, you grab a hold of the person next to you and scream your lungs out. You don't hold onto the person beside you, because they can stop the ride if something goes wrong. You hang on, because that person is your support as you experience the excitement of the rollercoaster. You share this exhilarating time together.

So, let me ask you a question. Who are you holding onto as you travel down the road to success? Do they support you through the twists, turns and flips? Do they enjoy hearing about your accomplishments and your plans to be free from the trials of life? If so, these people are your mastermind team. On the other hand, if you are surrounded by people that constantly put you down and have no desire to see you succeed, then it's time for a change. You need to make the decision to stop allowing those people to influence your life.

Imagine looking back over your life ten years from now, and you are still in the same exact place because someone in your life told you that you would never make it. They convinced you to give up! They didn't allow you to enjoy the challenge and achieve the freedom that you so desire. It's like standing in line for that rollercoaster, climbing into the seat and your friend decides to get in a different seat. You have no one to hold onto for support. Being alone on a rollercoaster for a few short minutes is nothing compared to being surrounded by people that don't support your dreams for the rest of your life. Make the decision to build a mastermind team that enjoys the challenge to change and gets excited about the thought of experiencing freedom in their lives.

I'm going to move right into the next letter in the word freedom. 'E' stands for encouragement. During hard times, it's easy to become frustrated and let the adversity win. Have you ever heard someone say "Well under the circumstances...?" That's a typical statement from a person that is simply overwhelmed by his current life situation and is letting the adversity control him instead of him taking control of the adversity. When you face something that seems unbearable, you need to encourage yourself and others around you that are experiencing the same hardship.

On January 2, 2006, a crew of thirteen men reported to work at Sago Coal Mine in West Virginia. As the men worked deeply in the mine, a tremendous explosion occurred and trapped the entire crew two miles below the Earth's surface. For forty-two painstaking hours, the world watched as rescuers desperately tried to save the men. When they finally reached the crew, twelve out of the thirteen were dead. The sole survivor, Randy McCloy, was pulled from the mine barely breathing but alive. He later shared his story about the turn of events on that day that would change his life forever.

The underground explosion knocked out the mine's electricity and left the men in complete darkness. With a limited supply of oxygen from their emergency air packs, the men hung a curtain to protect themselves from the thick smoke. Despite sharing their oxygen supply with each other, it wasn't long before their air supply ran out and the toxic fumes made it harder for them to breathe. Though worried and scared, the men began to accept their fate. They huddled together and began to pray. Some of the men wrote letters to their friends and families to express their final goodbyes.

Though faced with death, these men continued to encourage each other to the end. Some prolonged the life of a friend by sharing their oxygen supply. Another came up with the idea to write letters to their families just in case they didn't make it. They prayed together and were prepared to die together.

Inside the word encourage is courage. The men that perished in Sago Mine as well as the sole survivor, Randy McCloy, showed great courage as they faced the inevitable by encouraging not only each other but the families that they left behind. I once heard this quote that truly describes the great courage that these men showed during the greatest adversity that they had ever faced - *"Anyone can give up; it's the easiest thing in the world to do. But to hold it together when everyone else would understand if you fell apart, that's true strength"*.

It takes a lot of encouragement to achieve freedom in your life. That's why you want to attend personal development events, listen to positive materials, and build a supportive mastermind team. I encourage you to get absolutely focused on your freedom and set a date that you want to be free. It's called your "freedom date". You're no longer a slave to someone else's schedule or lifestyle. You are now manifesting, living and fulfilling your Why in life!

The next letter in the word freedom is the letter 'D'. It stands for dedication. Are you dedicated to what it takes to achieve freedom in your life? More importantly, are you dedicated to defending your freedom once you achieve it? Numerous wars have been fought to defend freedom, and millions of soldiers dedicated their lives to their countries during those wars. You're going to have a mental war in your own mind while you're pursuing freedom. The enemy will put thoughts in your head that you are not worthy of freedom, and you will begin to doubt yourself. If you are truly dedicated to achieving freedom, then you will combat those thoughts with positive affirmations. You will encourage yourself through the power of spoken words.

Here are a few to get you started:
- I am dedicated to achieving freedom in every area of my life.
- I am a dedicated to combating those doubts in my mind.
- I am dedicated to defending my freedom and know that I am worthy.

Dedication is a powerful characteristic. Most people are not dedicated and treat their freedom like it's owed to them. Those are the same type of people that sit around and complain about their lives instead of taking the action needed to change their situation. They are simply not dedicated to their Why. They're not dedicated to making decisions everyday that will put them one step closer to their freedom date.

It's awesome, because I know I am dedicated. I have dedicated my life to champions. I have dedicated my life to facing the struggles, developing strength, maintaining perseverance, and achieving the freedom that I deserve in my life. Can you say that about yourself? I challenge you to stare the enemy in its face and say, "Move out of my way, because I'm dedicated to my freedom!"

The next letter in the word freedom is 'O', which stands for obvious. Obvious is defined as easily seen, recognized or understood. It's obvious to me that you're a champion. Is it obvious to you? If so, then your belief should show in everything that you do and to everyone that you meet. When you enter a room, people should automatically see your confidence. It is obvious to them that nothing will stand in the way of you achieving your freedom.

It should be obvious that you're dedicated to going through the pain of change versus the pain of regret. It should be obvious that you are stretching yourself instead of remaining in your comfort zone. When people get to know you, are these things obvious about you? Unfortunately, most people are embarrassed to stand on faith and share their dreams with other people. They don't want to be laughed at or ridiculed. If this is you, then you don't want freedom bad enough. If you have to wear a mask around your friends and hide who you really are inside, then you aren't dedicated to being free. Instead, you are letting what others think about you dictate where you will go or what you will be in life.

One of my mentors is the great Rod Parsley. He is outspoken and takes a stand on what he believes. It's obvious that he believes in his mission and will stop at nothing to accomplish it. To no surprise, many people don't like him. They confuse his confidence with arrogance. They often say he's confused about the realities of the world. He's not confused. He's focused on achieving his Why in life, and it's obvious to everyone that nothing will stand in his way.

When you make the decision to become dedicated to achieving your freedom, you have a different look in your eye. You have different words coming out of your mouth. It will be obvious to people that you are a man (or woman) on a mission. You will stop engaging in waste of time activities and begin attending personal development events. You will associate with like-minded people that support your pursuit of happiness.

It will become obvious to everyone that you have taken control of your life.

I have a BONUS 'O' for you! This time, it stands for overcome. In order to be free, you must overcome every obstacle that gets in your way. One of the biggest obstacles that tends to destroy a person's dream isn't an actual thing, person or situation. It's fear of the unknown. When you begin your success journey, you can't be absolutely accurate in regards to what adversity you will face, the level of success that you will actually achieve or what date you will achieve your freedom. Yes, you have your freedom date in place but there is always that uncertainty of what's going to happen along the way.

While attending services at Christ Fellowship church in Palm Beach Gardens, Florida, I once heard Dr. Tom Mullins tell a story about a captain that led a very young group of troops into war. The young men were terrified about the unknown aspects such as what they would face when they encountered the enemy, if they would die, the strength of their opposition, etc. The captain knew that he had to come up with a way for his men to overcome their fears before they came face to face with the enemy. He took off his helmet and painted the back of it red so that his troops could see him and follow him through the battlefield. This decision made him an easy target for the enemy, but he risked his own life to help the young soldiers conquer their fears of the unknown by depending on his leadership to guide them through the battle.

The faith that lies inside your heart and your belief in yourself will serve as the painted red helmet that will guide you through your fear of the unknown. I believe that faith stands for *Find Answers In The Heart*. So when that fear tries to creep back into your life, dig down deep inside of your heart and take a giant step of faith towards your freedom.

The last letter in the word freedom is 'M', which stands for mountain, massive, move and momentum. Read this carefully. Massive momentum will move mountains in your life. You are almost at the end of your journey, and you can actually feel the sense of being free in every area of your life. All of a sudden, you look up and see this huge mountain blocking your path. This mountain is compiled of fear, doubt, naysayers and every other imaginable adversity. You gasp as it towers over you and wonder how you will possibly get around this thing.

That's when you pull yourself together and attack the mountain full force. You focus on your freedom, refuse to regret your decisions, enjoy the challenge, encourage yourself through affirmations, dedicate your strength to overcoming the obstacle, and make it obvious to that mountain that you aren't backing down. That's what I call building massive momentum. Remember, massive momentum will move mountains in your life. So shout it out...MOUNTAIN GET OUT OF MY WAY!

A category five hurricane doesn't start out as a destructive force. It begins as a storm, gains momentum and intensifies into a natural phenomenon that tears through the strongest structures that stand on this Earth. In contrast, you have to create this same type of massive momentum in your life by committing to daily action steps that will catapult you to the level of success. Commit to saying your affirmations, focusing on your freedom, associating with other champions and challenging yourself to change.

Now, let's recap the acronym for FREEDOM:

Focus – Get laser focused on your freedom.

Regret – Don't regret your decisions in life. Instead, face your fears and **Return** to your success journey knowing that nothing will stand in your way.

Enjoy – Enjoy the rollercoaster ride through life. Hold on tight to the person next to you and enjoy the twists, turns and flips that are ahead of you.

Encouragement – Speak words of encouragement into your life through affirmations and encourage others to achieve their dreams and goals.

Dedication – Be dedicated to achieving your freedom and remain dedicated to being free in your life once you've achieved it.

Obvious – Make it obvious to yourself and everyone that you encounter that you are focused and determined to be free. Bonus O – Overcome – In order to become free, you must overcome every obstacle that gets in your way

Massive **M**omentum to **M**ove **M**ountains – Commit to daily action steps that will create massive momentum in your life.

You can choose either to be free to make your own decisions or be a slave to the world for the rest of your life. I believe that you are a champion and worthy of all your dreams so take a step of faith and go for what you want in life…freedom.

Principle II
Know Who You Are

When you first meet someone, the typical conversation starter deals with who you are and what you do. Most people reply to those questions with answers like...I am Vice President of ABC Corporation or I am a homemaker or I am a sales manager for XYZ Company. Those responses are appropriate for explaining what you do, but are not truly representative of who you are. Remember, first impressions are everything so you need to make it clear exactly who and what you really are in life.

Let me give you an example. If someone asked me to tell them who I am, then I would say that I am an action-taking, fear-demolishing, eye-opening and mind-blowing champion. Why? Because that's who I really am. My business is Di Lemme Development Group, Inc. but that's not the core of who I am as an individual.

As a young child, you had no fear of telling anyone and everyone what you wanted to be in life. You believed with all of your heart that you could be anything that you wanted to be in life. Think about it...have you ever heard a child describe himself as the three year old son of Jane and John? No! He's more likely running through the house with a cape and mask yelling at the top of his lungs that he is a super hero that is going to save the world. So, what happens to that belief as you age? Most people find a job and simply become a fixture of that company. They allow the chain of command to dictate who they are in life. All sense of actual personal belief in who you really are as an individual slowly disappears.

In this teaching, I'm going to discuss eight uncomfortable, challenging, undeniable, uncompromising facts that will enable you to live the life of who you truly are within yourself. Why are these facts going to be uncomfortable, challenging, undeniable and uncompromising? If you choose to get uncomfortable and accept my challenge, then you cannot deny the fact that if you continue to compromise who you really are in life, then you'll go back to being known as a company title instead of the true champion that lies dormant within your heart.

Let me clarify that these eight facts will make you uncomfortable and challenge your beliefs about who you are as a person. Within the word challenge is change. You must be ready to accept the challenge to be uncomfortable so that you can finally make a change in your life that will allow you to go to the next level. I truly believe that the following facts will enable you to live, manifest and create the life that you have the right to live.

Fact #1: Your ears are your faith gates. There are many gated communities throughout the United States. Typically, mostly upper middle class and wealthier people live in these neighborhoods. In addition to their home security systems, living in a gated community is another way for these people to prevent thieves from stealing what they've worked so hard for in life. Unless you have the entry code or provide the correct information to the security, you will not be allowed to enter the neighborhood.

Similarly, you have to treat your ears like security gates that are protecting you from the garbage that tries to enter your mind. To do this, you must analyze what you're listening to on a daily basis especially the background noise in your office, home and car. How many times have you turned on the television while you cleaned house, worked on your computer or had dinner with your family? Most people don't realize that their unconscious mind is focusing on that background noise and taking in every negative word.

Not only are you unconsciously feeding your mind garbage, studies have shown that children growing up in an environment where the television is always on may suffer in speech development and social interaction. If you have to have something playing in the background at all times, wouldn't it make more sense to turn on some inspirational music or pop in a motivational CD or DVD? Reach up and grab your ears. Yes, this sounds silly but do it anyway. Grab your ears. As you see, they are attached to your body and you own them. It's time for you to exercise your ownership rights and decide what you allow to enter your ears.

Romans 10:17 says "Faith comes by hearing, and hearing by the Word." If you are constantly hearing negative conversation, depressing news on television, etc., then how do you expect to receive the faith that you will need to achieve your Why in life? Your ears are not only like security gates that keep the negativity out, but also your faith gates that allow the positive material into your ears that will build faith in your heart.

I have a huge high definition television on my desk. However, I don't watch the news or any other negative nonsense on it. I turn up my surround sound and watch inspirational stations. That's right...I have teachers like Kenneth and Gloria Copeland, Rod Parsley, John Hagee, Joel Osteen, Creflo Dollar and Dr. Tom Mullins pumping through my speakers twenty four hours a day. Even when I'm on coaching calls or writing at my desk, I have motivational messages lightly playing. I am flooding my faith gates with positive, empowering messages.

I was born and raised in Yonkers, New York and my wife was raised in rural Tennessee. I have a very strong New York accent and she sounds like she just walked off a farm. Why? Because we were raised by parents with the same accents and grew up around others that sounded just like us. Your accent comes from what you hear from birth through your developmental stages of childhood. Basically, the sounds that we heard as children eventually flowed freely from our mouths. Our early opinions and ideas about the world are also formed by what we heard from our family and friends.

This doesn't simply stop once we reach adulthood. Whatever or whoever you are listening to everyday will determine who you are as a person. It also determines the level of faith in your heart. Remember, faith comes by hearing. If you are constantly speaking gloom and doom and have no idea how you could possibly achieve your dreams in life, then take a good look at who and what you are listening to.

I'll be very direct. It irritates me when I meet people that proclaim to be professionals in the personal development industry, but negative words flow out of their mouths like water raging over Niagara Falls. Their words do not match what they claim to be. I've devoted my life to assisting others with achieving success, and I focus daily on my Why in life. With that known, would it make any sense for me to go throughout my day complaining, moaning and groaning? No, that's foolish. But so many people do just that. They claim to be one thing and then act like another.

This clearly proves that what goes into your ears comes out of your mouth. I doubt those same people are listening to inspirational, motivational material on a daily basis. I doubt they even think about protecting their "faith gates" by refusing to listen to negative garbage.

Now, take a long, hard look at yourself. Is this you? Do you talk one way and then walk another?

Imagine if you recorded the words that came out of your mouth for just one full day. What would that recording sound like? I can promise you that the words that come out of your mouth will match the material that is going into your ears. Whatever you allow to enter your faith gates will program your heart, spirit and mind to reveal who you really are as a person.

You don't learn this in school or usually in your home. I know that I didn't. I have great parents and a supportive family yet I didn't learn about developing my faith gates. Now, I read the Bible a lot and it finally hit me when I read that *faith comes by hearing and hearing of the Word.* I knew at that moment in my heart that I had to flood my faith gates with positive affirmations, success oriented words and powerful teachings from people that have done what I want to do in life.

Let's commit. I'm giving you eight challenges so this is the first one. I challenge you to turn off the negative background noise and flood your ears (faith gates) with positive material for thirty days. You have to agree that you won't compromise on this challenge in which you will refuse to allow any negative conversation, music, television or any other form of media to enter your faith gates. You must also listen to the words coming out of your mouth. Do they represent who you really are?

Remember, whatever goes into your ears will come out of your mouth. It's time to challenge yourself to change!

Fact 2: It's more important to look at the windshield than to stare in the rear view mirror. The majority of people drive a car or have at least been in a car so you can envision this comparison. The rear view mirror is very small, and typically you spend less than five percent of your driving time looking behind you. However, your windshield is huge, because you must have clarity and visibility in front of you to be able to drive your car and arrive at your destination safely. The number one rule of driving is to always keep your eyes on the road, and a clear windshield is extremely important.

What does this have to do with success? I'm going to answer that question with a serious question for you. Are you more focused on what lies behind you in your rear view mirror or what is ahead of you as you stare out the windshield of your life? One of the most common excuses that I hear is how a person's past is preventing them from being successful. They continue to look back at their past and dwell on things that happened long ago. It's as if they are driving a car and looking back in their rear view mirror instead of focusing on what's ahead of them. They continue to run off the road, hit the guard rails and crash into adversity.

Many people introduce themselves to me and immediately say things like "I am a recovering alcoholic…I am a sexual abuse victim…I am learning disabled…I am divorced." It's time for you to stop allowing your past or something that has happened to you in the past dictate who you are in life. Don't get me wrong. I'm not undermining what horrible things might have occurred in your life, but I refuse to allow you to believe that those things make up who you are as a person.

It's time for you to stop looking in the rear view mirror and focus on the road ahead of you. If you do this, then you won't be continually questioning what impact your past has on your ability to achieve success. Your mental mindset will focus on the clear windshield ahead of you and see a road of endless possibilities.

It seems like everywhere I go I hear things like…"I used to be healthy. I used to be in great shape. I used to give money away. I used to tithe. I used to go to church. I used to listen to motivational material. I used to be excited about life." This is simply a person's way of reflecting back on their past when times were good and using it as an excuse on why they are failing now.

Instead of talking about the good ol' days and how you used to be, start speaking words of empowerment about who you believe that you are today. Say these affirmations out loud:

- I am a giver!

- I am listening to inspirational material!
- I am prosperous in every area of my life!
- I am surrounded by people that love me!
- I am a champion!

Now, doesn't that sound better than moaning and groaning about what you used to be. Even if you aren't prosperous in every area of your life, speak the words out loud and start believing that's who you are. Don't let your past steal your dreams of becoming who you want to be in life.

Let me give you another example. Imagine getting into your car, fastening your seatbelt and preparing to go to the grocery store. Now, imagine that you look up and your rear view mirror is the size of your windshield and the windshield is the size of your rear view mirror. You suddenly realize that you can't even get out of your parking spot even to travel a few miles to the grocery store. You are unable to reach your destination, because the massive rear view mirror (your past) is making it impossible for you to focus on the tiny windshield to see road in front of you (your future).

It's time for you to accept challenge number two. I want you to commit to stop looking in your rear view mirror and start focusing on what lies ahead of you. Isn't it refreshing to know that your past doesn't define who you are today? I also want you to commit to saying who you are instead of what you used to be. Write out your affirmations and read them out loud everyday until you believe that you are who you say you are.

Fact #3: The channel that you are tuned into will determine your future. There are two channels on TV that I find amazing - the Discovery Channel and the History Channel. Both of these channels provide amazing information that took years to compile. Their researchers have literally traveled back in time to discover unbelievable facts about the world and often dedicate their lives to validating these facts through more intensive discovery methods.

When you are trying to figure out who you are in life, you should exert as much time and energy in your research as the professionals behind the programs on the Discovery Channel and History Channel. You will tune into your very own Champion Channel to find out exactly what makes you different from everyone else and why you will be able to achieve your Why in life.

This will be no easy task. First, you will need to excavate the champion that lies within your heart. It is buried under layers of procrastination and fear that have built up over the years as you've become complacent in your current lifestyle. Think back...Do you remember when you were excited about your goals and dreams? You had plans of being prosperous and living life to the fullest. That champion mindset still lives inside of you!

After uncovering your inner champion, sit down and write out your Why in life. Your Why is basically the reason why you get out of bed every day. It's your purpose for living. It truly defines who you are. You are basically rediscovering yourself. Here's an example of a Why that was written by one of my coaching students:

"I am dealing with all the challenges of building my business today, because my WHY is to spend more time with my family, provide for my children's education, and have the finances needed to take regular family vacations and be a mentor to my kids. I am donating/tithing a percentage of my earnings to my church or favorite organization. I am making a difference today as a profit producing, fear demolishing, record breaking, action taking, fired up and laser focused champion."

Isn't that powerful? Your Why should be clear and concise. It should tell someone who you are and where you are going. There's no room for doubt or fear. It must be a statement that declares what you are, not what you want to be.

Now that you've completed the discovery phase by extracting the champion out of your heart and writing out your detailed Why in life, it's time for you to prove it. Remember, I said that you would be like the researchers on the History Channel and Discovery Channel. After an

Just like Nehemiah, you must build a wall to protect yourself from the enemy. Your enemy isn't a physical warrior from another land. It is procrastination, fear, naysayers, negative associations and other adversities that try to stop you from achieving your Why in life. Your mastermind team will be the workers that help you design the wall and stand at the weak spots where the enemy typically tries to attack. They will believe in you and encourage you along the way. The bricks in your wall are made of faith, motivation, courage, belief and perseverance. You will work vigorously until your wall is completed, and no enemy can infiltrate your Why.

This all sounds great, but if you don't strengthen your wall everyday by immersing yourself in personal development, then cracks form in your walls. Weeds will begin to grow through the cracks and insects will enter as the cracks spread through the foundation. The negativity of the outside world will slowly seep in, and you will start doubting yourself and your ability to achieve your Why in life. It isn't long before your wall becomes weakened by decay and succumbs to the enemy.

This is often the result when people hang out with negative friends, read gossip magazines instead of inspirational material and watch garbage television shows instead of feeding their minds with motivational messages. If you find yourself falling back into old habits and your wall begins to crumble, then it's time for you to separate yourself from the madness and start secretly rebuilding your wall that protects your dream from the enemy.

The wall that protects my belief in who I am and my ability to achieve my Why in life is solid as the rock that Nehemiah used to build the wall of Jerusalem. The bricks of my wall are made of integrity and faith. I strengthen my wall everyday by reading the Bible and immersing myself in motivational material. I refuse to allow the enemy to discourage me or weaken my wall of faith.

It's time for your fourth challenge. Take your time with this one and don't move forward with the reading until this challenge is completed. I want you to go to a quiet place and evaluate your current life situation. Now, devise a plan to build your wall. What are your bricks made of? Who is on the mastermind team that will help you build your wall and stand at your weak spots when the enemy attacks? Make a list of the adversities (the enemies) that your wall will keep out.

The final step is the most important. What daily action steps will you take to strengthen your wall? This great wall will explode your belief in who you are and your limitless abilities to achieve your Why in life.

Fact #5: The most dangerous person in your life might be your best friend. As you read that statement, I know that you got a little bit angry. You are saying to yourself, "My best friend isn't dangerous.

She supports me through thick and thin. She would never hurt me." Are you sure about that?

One of the biggest reasons that people remain anchored to their past instead of moving forward towards their future is their associations. They change everything in their lives including their bad habits, negative thinking and poor decision-making but continue to hang out with the same group of people. More often than not, these so-called friends are the chains that are keeping you shackled to your past. They have no desire to change their lives so why would you think that want you to better yourself?

The majority of these people will not intentionally hurt you. It's their actual character traits and their habits that will have a negative effect on your life. So, what do these people look like? Most of them don't have a certain look, but they do have many of the following traits:

- Constantly speak negative words
- See no light at the end of the tunnel
- Allow failure to be an option
- Don't believe in dreams (yours or theirs)
- Want to "make" money rather than "earn" it
- Always have an opinion that focuses on the negative
- Become complacent in their lives and are satisfied with it
- Make decisions that result in failure 99% of the time

Have you ever heard the old saying, "Pigs don't know pigs stink?" Basically, it means that you don't even realize that you are hanging out with people that are going nowhere in life, because you haven't stepped outside your circle of influence to take a look from the outside. If you did, you would likely see your friends rolling around in the same old pig pen day in and day out. Talking about the same slop that they have talked about for years and allowing their trashy view of the world to dictate their success or lack of it.

Is that harsh? Yes, but it's the truth. How do you expect to become who you believe that you are in life if you hang out with people that are constantly pushing you off the mountain when you reach the top? Here's an eye-opening exercise for you. Take a look at the last ten people that you dialed on your cellular phone or home phone if you don't have a cell phone. Think of all of their daily habits, yearly incomes, relationships, goals and overall success in life. Now, average those things out. Do you like what you see? I hope so, because that's where you will be in five years if you don't change your current associations.

If you are in the small percentage of people in the world that have a great mastermind team that is made up of positive, supportive individuals, then kudos to you. Unfortunately, most people don't fall into that category. Most people are surrounded by so-called friends that are holding them back from achieving their Why in life. Do you have these people on your Mastermind Team? If so, what are you going to do about it? You have two choices.

You can allow those people to control YOUR destiny with their negative opinions, failure mindset and inability to dream.
OR
You can love them, leave them and show them. What does that mean? You simply continue to care for them as a friend, associate, etc., but you no longer allow them to negatively impact your life.

If they don't like attending personal development seminars, then don't invite them. If they don't like your positive mastermind team members, then stop allowing them to join your mastermind team gatherings. How do you show them? You forge forward towards the achievement of your Why despite any obstacle that you encounter. Those people will start to see that you are serious and nothing will stop you!

Here's your fifth challenge. Write this down - I am going to stop allowing others to steal my dream. I am leaving my negative associations behind. I am building a mastermind team of true champions that believe in me and my dream. I want you to confirm that to your spirit by saying it out loud over and over until you believe it.

Fact #6: Your health is the result of your decisions. I exercise every single day. I also drink a gallon of water with a half a cup of lemon juice everyday. No matter where I am in the world, I exercise and drink my water. Why? Because I made a decision to be healthy.

I could not have my wealth if I did not have my health. I want you to truly understand that. This is the missing link for most people. You have big dreams and want to accomplish success in every area of your life, but this is simply unattainable if you don't have the physical and mental energy to do it. Some people push their body to the extreme and still achieve their goals, but they are rarely around long enough after they achieve success to actually enjoy it. I don't call that success. I call that ignorance.

You can have all the wealth in the world, but if you're not keeping yourself healthy by feeding your body the right food and maintaining a regular exercise regimen, then it isn't worth a dime. Why would you want to be rich if you are too miserable to enjoy it? Whether you want to believe it or not, your level of health plays a great part in defining who you are as a person.

If you are one of those people that say "I can't afford to join a gym or buy expensive fruit and vegetables." Stop it! I didn't say that you had to join a gym. Simply put on your sneakers and take a walk. That's free. There are many exercises that you can do outdoors or within your home that don't cost a dime so that excuse doesn't work anymore. It is also foolish to say that you can't afford to eat healthy. Fruits and vegetables are typically less expensive than those sugary snacks that are filling your pantry or the greasy fast food that you are eating on your way home from work at least three times a week. Being healthy isn't an expensive habit, but it will cost you your life if you don't make the decision to be healthy.

Despite Americans spending billions of dollars per year on diet and exercise, a recent study shows that only about one in seven adults in America engage in regular physical activity. **A July 2007 study from the Johns Hopkins Bloomberg School of Public Health estimates that seventy-five percent of American adults and twenty-four percent of American children will be overweight or obese by 2015. This is a horrible reality that can be drastically reduced by a person's decision to eat healthy and exercise.**

You probably aren't going to like challenge number six, but I don't care because it's for your own good. I want you to make a decision to get healthy. That includes exercising and eating right. Set fitness goals for yourself. Join a gym. Exercise with friends. Visit the local fruit and vegetable market instead of the bakery. There are many ways to develop a healthy lifestyle. Find the ways that suit you and stick to them.

Decide to be healthy and live to enjoy your success. I can't wait to see the before and after pictures!

Fact #7: Rest prepares your body and mind for life's daily challenges. The Bible describes how David, one of the greatest warriors in the Bible, rested every night to get ready for battle the next day. Sleep refreshes your body and mind so that you can focus and make decisions with clarity.

T.D. Jakes has a great teaching that describes how the enemy wins when you're weary. Without rest, you can't think straight. You make bad decisions. You say bad words. You associate with bad people. You are completely unable to fully control your life, because you are too tired and frustrated to deal with it. That's when the enemy attacks! You begin to question your own abilities and doubt yourself in every situation. However, this entire situation can be avoided. Simply, choose to get an adequate amount of rest.

Personally, I need eight hours of sleep per night to be at my best the next day. Of course there are many medical opinions about this topic, but most recommend between six to eight hours per night. I truly believe that it's a personal choice. For instance, I have a friend in Malta named Alfred that only sleeps between three to five hours per night. It seems to work for him, but I don't recommend it for everyone. So, how much is enough? Medically speaking... I have no clue. If you roll out of bed in the morning with a clear mind and rested body, then I say that's a great start.

Your failure to get enough rest not only affects you but also everyone else around you. Have you ever tried to have a serious conversation when you were just too tired to think straight? Your judgment goes out the window and you likely give in to the demands of others. Possibly, you've been working on an important project and cut corners because you are simply too fatigued to give it your best. These are situations in which others suffer from your lack of rest.

You can't deny the fact you feel better when you get a great night's sleep. Your seventh challenge is pretty simple. Sleep. That's it. Instead of turning on the television to watch mindless shows, going out to late-night hangouts with friends or continually staying up late to finish a project, get into your bed and go to sleep. You can't be the person that you want to be in life and accomplish all of your dreams and goals unless you are able to be mentally and physically prepared so make sleep a priority beginning today.

Fact #8: When one door closes, another one opens. Yes, I'm sure that you've all heard this at least a thousand times but I want to give you a new spin on this old saying. Here it is...you must close someone in order to open up a long-term relationship with that person.

Most likely, you are in some type of business. You may be an author, a speaker, in network marketing, selling real estate or simply in general business. No matter what type of business you are in or where you are in your life, you must be a closer. If you meet someone that you know would be a great asset to your business, then take the time to explain to him why he should join your team, company, etc. You must close him on the facts about who you are and where you are going in life in order to open up a long-term relationship with him.

If you want something in life, then you have to go after it. It's not different in business. To close someone, basically means to show that person beyond a shadow of a doubt that becoming part of your business, mastermind team, company, etc. will change their life. It's a decisive step that will lead to solid relationships.

When you leave an event or business meeting without making an effort to expand yourself and your business, then you have left doors open for other people, likely your competition, to walk through. Show your strength and belief in who you are as a person by cementing that new business partner.

Yes, it is uncomfortable to be so confident but it will explode not only your business but your circle of influence. When you surround yourself with people that become part of your life with a clear understanding of who you are and where you are going, there are no gray areas. The majority of misconceptions are cleared up in the initial closing process. You will have to build upon those relationships, but you set a standard for yourself and your business partners and/or team members from the very beginning.

No matter whether you like him or hate him, Donald Trump is one of the greatest closers today. He once said *"If you have to lie, cheat or steal, you're just not doing it right...My career is a model of tough, fair dealing and fantastic success without shortcuts and without breaking the law."* I have no doubt that all of Donald Trump's business partners know exactly where they stand in their relationship with him, because he closed them in the very beginning on who he was and what he expected.

You don't necessarily have to be as abrasive as Donald Trump, but you do have to have the same type of belief in who you are and what you will accomplish. Whoever you meet must be able to detect your inner strength and not question your belief in yourself or your business. The last challenge for you is to become a closer. This will likely take some time because you will have to build your confidence to the point that when you are sitting in front of a potential business partner or mastermind team member there are no qualms about who you are and where you are going. Are you strong enough to do this? I truly believe that you are.

I told you from the very beginning that these eight facts were going to be uncomfortable, challenging, undeniable, and uncompromising. However, I also told you that these facts will enable you to live the life of who you truly are within yourself. If you accept the eight challenges that I gave you and stop compromising on who you are as a person to fit some type of societal mold, then your life will change forever. The champion inside of you will emerge and the world will know that you…the person that you really are…has arrived.

Principle III
Understand Feelings versus Emotions

Have you ever heard of Friday Night Fights? It's basically a weekly fight night in which two great boxers go head to head in the ring to see who is the better fighter. Many times, it is a battle to the very end. The same type of fierce battle often happens between your feelings and your emotions. However, this isn't a weekly fight for you. It's a lifelong fight!

Most people enter this ring on a daily basis struggling back and forth with the decision to go with their feelings about a particular situation or with their gut instinct that tells them to go for it no matter what. When people are led by their feelings, their mind starts telling them that they don't feel like getting uncomfortable, they don't feel like taking action, they don't feel like prospecting, they don't feel like closing, they don't feel like stretching themselves and so on. As a direct result, ninety-seven percent of people are dead broke by the age of sixty-five, because they don't stretch themselves beyond their feelings and delve into their true emotions.

A gut instinct is a person's true emotion about a situation that they are facing. This emotion is driven by the faith that lies in your heart. This faith often tells you to take a chance and believe in yourself. American film critic Roger Ebert once said, "Your intellect may be confused, but your emotions will never lie to you." Sometimes your emotions flood your heart so heavily that it's undisputable what you should do in a particular situation. At that very moment, you sense a gut instinct that tells you to step out in faith. Then the battle begins. Your feelings step in and offer you an easier path or shortcut.

Here's a reality check. You are exactly where you are today in life, because you either made the decision to act on your true emotions OR you were driven by your feelings to remain comfortable and take the easier path. Many times, I hear people say that they will see how they feel about the situation after thinking it over. These people don't believe in faith. Since they can't see it or touch it, they simply choose not to believe in it. I try to explain to these individuals that faith is like gravity. You can't feel or see gravity, but you won't challenge it. You won't go jump off a building to prove that gravity doesn't exist. Yes, that's foolish but so is not having the belief in yourself to step out in faith.

In the battle between feelings and emotions, you will always lose if you bet on feelings. What does that mean? Your emotions are developed over time and rest on a solid foundation called your belief system. This system is made up of your morals, faith, integrity, and courage. It gives you the ability to reach deep within yourself and believe that you are capable of achieving things that may seem impossible to others.

Your feelings are very different because they are based on what you think about something. Unlike emotions, feelings are on the surface and typically flow out of our mouths without much thought. We often see this happen when someone is offended by another person and becomes defensive. This person will lash out and spew words of anger, because their feelings were hurt. The person later regrets what he said, because how he acted isn't truly representative of who he is as a person. He reacted on his initial feelings about the situation instead of taking the time to reach deep into his emotions to determine how he should handle it.

On September 11, 2001, I rolled out Di Lemme Development Group, Inc. My excitement had been building about this day for a long time. I put a lot of hard work into structuring my company, compiling materials and developing the website. Needless to say, I hit the ground running that morning. I was immediately stopped in my tracks when I heard that an airplane just hit the World Trade Center. I immediately turned on the television to watch this horrific terrorist attack unfold.

It was obvious that day wasn't the day for celebration. It has actually been called the saddest day in American history. Based on those facts alone, it would have been easy for me to give into my feelings and postpone the birth of Di Lemme Development Group, Inc. However, I took some time to myself and decided to step out in faith. As an American entrepreneur, I felt that it was my duty to forge forward towards my dreams. I refused to allow the enemy to dictate my future because of how I was feeling that very day.

My first electronic magazine (ezine) was sent out on September 14, 2001. There were only a few people in my database at that time, and most were family and friends. I kept calling my father to see if he received the ezine, because I wasn't getting any responses. I swallowed my pride and continued to send out the weekly emails to my database.

Not long after that, I began hosting Monday Night Millionaire Motivational Tele-Classes. In the beginning, the only people on the call were a few of my colleagues, my fiancé and some family members. For the first forty-five minutes, I would teach a motivational lesson and the last fifteen minutes were devoted to questions from my listening audience. Thank God my friends and family stuck by me during those times and graciously asked questions to fill the dead air.

Let's just say that the first few months seemed hopeless, and I didn't really feel like sending out ezines or doing those tele-classes anymore. I knew that I had the credibility to be a business coach and motivational speaker so why weren't more people coming aboard. This heartache made me more determined than ever. I learned to listen to my gut and follow my instincts (emotions). It wasn't long before I began receiving feedback from champions around the world about my ezine, and the continuous beeps on the tele-class line let me know that I had more than ten people on the call. It all finally came together, because my emotions overpowered my feelings.

We all have dreams within our hearts. Unfortunately, not everyone has the courage to listen to their heart, step out in faith and go after their dreams. I made the decision to achieve my dream. No one did it for me. Yes, I had a great mastermind team that supported my decision but I was the only one that could make it happen. It was one of the scariest times in my life, but I knew if I didn't follow my heart that I would never achieve my Why in life. The time has come for you to go after what you really want in life. Create a plan of action and take that step of faith towards your dreams.

Let me break this to you gently…not everyone will support your dreams. Even when you begin to have a significant amount of success, you will still have those people that simply don't believe in you. Unfortunately, it will likely be some of your closest family and friends. Their actions and words of disbelief will hurt your feelings, but you have to turn to your emotions and deal with that disappointment without letting it affect your level of success.

My company had just gotten off the ground, and I was enjoying the level of success that I had achieved thus far. That's when it happened for me…I ran into an old friend. She just couldn't believe that

John Di Lemme, the former stutterer, had achieved any type of goals especially in the world of personal development. She acted as if I were lying to her. I was foolish to even try to offer her any type of proof, because it didn't matter anyway. Her failure to believe that I was living my dreams wasn't about proof. It was the fact that she simply didn't believe in me or my abilities.

Finally, I had enough. I looked her directly in the eyes and said "I know you can't believe it, but I believe it because inside unbelievable is believable. Inside impossible is possible. Inside procrastination is action. Inside self-doubt is belief. Guess what? I am just beginning. I have just begun the process of changing people's lives worldwide." I didn't respond with feelings that I had about what she was saying to me. If I did, it would have been a lot of harsh words that I wouldn't have been proud of saying. Instead, I relied on my strong foundation of belief in myself and told her exactly why I deserved to achieve my dreams just like everyone else.

I stood up and took control of the enemy. No, I don't mean that she's personally the enemy, but the words that she was speaking over my life were the enemy. Negative words about your goals and dreams are like daggers in your heart. If you don't have full faith in yourself and what you can achieve, then words are the greatest obstacle that you will face. It's like the old saying "Sticks and stones will break my bones, but words will never hurt me." I'm here to tell you that is a complete lie. Words, especially from those closest to you, can knock you right off the mountain top that you worked so hard to climb. It's your responsibility to stand on your strong foundation of belief and hold up your shield of faith in order to prevent the enemy from stealing your dreams.

In the beginning, you won't feel like doing what you know needs to be done. Believe me when I say that it was completely miserable in the beginning when I wasn't having much success. There were days that I wanted to give up, but that little flame of faith in my heart kept me going. However, that is the most important part of the process, because you are laying the foundation.

Close your eyes and imagine the foundation of a house being laid. If that cement foundation isn't solid, then the house will collapse. Jesus used this same illustration in Matthew 7:24-27 when he said, "Anyone who listens to my teaching and follows it is wise, like a person who builds a house on solid rock. Though the rain comes in torrents and the floodwaters rise and the winds beat against that house, it won't collapse because it is built on bedrock. But anyone who hears my teaching and doesn't obey it is foolish, like a person who builds a house on sand. When the rains and floods come and the winds beat against that house, it will collapse with a mighty crash."

As you begin to lay your foundation of belief and build upon your dreams, you will likely be easily distracted by naysayers. This is a test for you. That's why it's important to approach that type of negativity head-on and stay strong. Don't get irritated by these types of obstacles and allow your feelings to take over. Instead, treat the obstacle as an opportunity to become stronger in what you believe about yourself and your dreams.

Let me ask you a few questions...Are you really in it for the long haul? Are you willing to commit to building a strong foundation and overcoming the obstacles that get in your way? Will you be able to handle the enemy through your emotions rather than allowing your feelings to take control? Here's a tough question for you - What's at stake if you don't at least try to accomplish your dreams? Are you prepared to live the rest of your life without knowing if it were really possible?

It's easy to give up and simply go back to what you were comfortable doing. For me, I could have just gone back to the art gallery, worked every day and ended up with a good salary at the end of the week. However, this wasn't an option for me, because I wanted more. I knew that there was more out of life than just living a mediocre existence from day to day. I had things that I wanted to accomplish in my life, and I was prepared to risk everything just to have the opportunity to achieve those things.

Now, let's say that I ran into that same person that questioned my ability to achieve my goals in the very beginning stages five years later. There's a twist. Let's pretend for a minute that I gave up. What would I say to her when she asked me about the business that I had stood up for and believed in five years earlier? What would my excuse be? I gave up, because certain people told me it wouldn't work. I couldn't find people who would be interested in finding their Why, internalizing the power of their dream, understanding the million dollar training series or learning how to build a multi-million dollar network marketing business. I couldn't find anybody to attend an event. I couldn't find anybody who wanted to listen to me. What do you think she would have said? Probably something like, "I told you so." More importantly, how would I have felt? I can think of one word...DEFEATED.

Jump back to reality. I didn't give up, and there's no way that I would let the enemy defeat me in the fight for my dreams. Let's cross the same bridge into your heart. I want you to focus right now and listen to your heart when you answer this question. How are you going to deal with your true emotions when somebody asks you about a dream that you gave up on? I'm not talking about those feelings that will flare up and make you want to punch that person out. I'm referring to the emotions in your heart that are telling you that it isn't anyone else's fault but your own. At that point, you will realize that you allowed the enemy to win and your dreams are no longer possible because you gave up.

What would you do if you found yourself in that situation? Take back your dreams from the enemy, stand strong on your foundation of belief and ignite that flame of faith in your heart. What if that same person asked you about your dream after you took it back from the enemy? Wouldn't it feel good to tell that person – "I'm phenomenal, better than ever, and living my dreams!" You could really get crazy and say – "I am an achiever! I am a champion! I am focused! I am bombarding fear! I am taking action!" Now, those are some fired-up emotions. Let your emotions move you. Inside the word, emotion is motion. Allow your emotions to be the motion that pushes you straight to the top.

People may think that you are crazy and in some type of cult. Just laugh and agree. Tell them that you have lost your mind and gained the mind of a champion. Explain that you are in a cult – a culture of success that will catapult you to the next level in your life. If you really want to freak them out, tell them all about your dreams and what you believe that you will accomplish. This isn't bragging. It's just simply letting them know where you are going and what you are doing. If they aren't along for the ride, then tell them to get off the boat!

To maintain this momentum and build upon the emotions that support your success journey, you must build a dream wall. Cover an entire wall or a small space in your home or office that you look at the most throughout your day with things that encompass your dream. If you want to be able to tithe $50,000 to your church, then write it out and put it up on your dream wall. If you want to be a speaker, then cut out a picture of yourself and put it on your dream wall beside other great speakers from around the world. You have to see it to believe it. Speak your future into existence and get emotional about it. Be faithful in your decisions to go for your dreams. After all, faith is the secret of all goal achievers and Why fulfillers.

I was a stutterer and now I'm a fear demolishing, profit producing, income generating, worldwide life-changing international motivational speaker and strategic business coach. You better believe it took a lot of faith for me to even begin to believe that I could achieve. My dream wall was huge when I first started and got bigger as I accomplished goal after goal. Right now, my dream wall covers the walls in my construction zone, known as office to most people. Office has a negative connotation plus I am building my dreams in that room so why not call it my construction zone.

You've got to receive your dream! The word "receive" in the old Greek means to take a hold of with an aggressive attitude. When it comes to your dream in life, you've got to receive it and take a hold of it like an aggressive pit bull. It's yours and you refuse to let anyone take it away from you!

I had the opportunity to meet Olympian Randy Snow. As you know, Olympians are dedicated to their sport and endure strenuous training in order to be the very best that they can be. They visualize themselves bowing their heads as a medal is draped around their necks. Excellence is a way of life for these champions. However, Randy Snow had one major obstacle to overcome on his quest for the gold. At the age of sixteen, Randy was working on a farm when a one thousand pound bale of hay fell on him leaving him paralyzed from the waist down. Instead of using his disability as an excuse, he went after his dream with a vengeance. Randy achieved the prestigious title of gold medalist and is considered one the greatest gold medal wheelchair athletes in history. In 2004, Randy Snow was the first Paralympian inducted into the United States Olympic Hall of Fame.

But what if he had given up after his accident? It would have definitely been understandable for him to doubt his abilities and simply say that he didn't feel like training, practicing, competing, etc. Even with his adversity, Randy Snow fought for his dream of being an Olympian. This man is a prime example that anyone can do anything they set their mind to when there is a burning desire in their heart. Excuses are for failures! One of the biggest excuses is "I don't feel..."

I've had so many people tell me "John, I don't feel like prospecting. I don't feel like listening to personal development material. I don't feel like attending motivational seminars. I don't feel like hanging out with my mastermind team." Well, you know what...I don't care about how you are feeling right now. I am more concerned about how you are going to feel five years from today when somebody asks you what's going on with your business and you tell them that you quit. How will that feel? Did you feel that ache in your heart when I made that statement?

They're going to laugh at you and say "I told you so". They don't have the right to do that! You have the birthright to achieve massive success. Read this over and over and over and understand that they don't have the right to steal your dream. You have the right to fulfill your dream.

Here's what I want you to do right now. Make a list of the people in your life that try to steal your dreams. They make you feel bad about yourself and foolish for trying to achieve your goals. After speaking with these individuals, you simply have no motivation to do anything productive. Their negativity makes you dwell on your "surface" feelings that cast doubt on your abilities. Your focus shifts to not believing that you can achieve your dreams. Don't listen to them! Instead, dig down deep in your heart and release your true emotions that drive you to accomplish your goals. That's where that little champion lives inside of you that is dying to get out and conquer the world.

Allow those emotions to take over when fear tries to creep into your life. Yes, I said LIFE. Your goals and dreams have to be what you live for and not just some small segment of your life. If not, how do you expect to ever really achieve them? Do you think Randy Snow became a gold medalist by only focusing on sports two percent of the time? No, that's ridiculous. Then why do people think that they can build a million dollar business when they devote absolutely no time to developing the foundation of their business? It doesn't just happen overnight without any commitment!

Many of you reading this right now have been at the ninety-nine yard line of quitting. After all, it's easier to quit than face your adversity head on. When you get to this point and you are about to cross that line, just imagine me grabbing you by the back of your jersey like a football coach and pulling you back in the game. Are you at the point of giving up right now? If so, close your eyes and visualize me grabbing you by your shirt collar, looking in your eyes and telling you that I love your dream. That's right...I LOVE YOUR DREAM! If you love your dream as much as I do, then agree with me and say out loud – "I love my dream!" When two or more come together, there's a spirit of achievement that breaks all barriers.

I refuse to give up on you so don't you quit on me! Remember, you have to get emotional about your dream. It will likely take blood, sweat and tears along with a lot of ups and downs. But that's what it takes. You've got to get down and dirty in your dream. Look into your kids' eyes or your spouse's eyes. Better yet, look right into a mirror at yourself. When those eyes are staring back at you, do you fully understand why it is your responsibility to achieve your dream? Can you imagine looking into those same eyes knowing that you gave up on your dream? You simply can't allow that to happen!

Now, take a look at that list of people (aka dream stealers) that you wrote down earlier. Understand those are your roadblocks. If you want your dream bad enough and are determined to achieve it, then you have to stop listening to those people. If not, their words will kill your dream. Have you ever heard that old saying "Sticks and stones will break my bones, but words will never hurt me?" That's one of the biggest lies out there. You can heal from physical wounds, but words can annihilate your belief in yourself and your dream long-term or even indefinitely.

I see it all the time at events especially my boot camps. People get emotional about their dream and vow that today is the day that things will change. Within that emotion is motion that gets their hearts moving in the right direction. At that moment, they truly believe that they can do it and they understand what's at risk if they fail. Most people keep the momentum going for a few days or weeks at the most, and then it happens. They settle back in their old routine and start listening to their negative friends and family. Those emotions that filled their heart are buried beneath doubt and fear once again.

On a more positive note, there is the three percent crowd. These are the people that leave the event emotionally fired-up and refuse to let anything or anyone get in the way of their dream. They stand out from the crowd! We all know those type of people that just have something about them that make you take a second look. I am fortunate to have several students around the world that have this trait. So, why do they stand out? It's simple. They made the decision to allow their emotion to drive them instead of letting their feelings get in the way. I've never once heard these students say that they didn't feel like doing something. Now, I'm not saying that they never have those days. But when they do, they don't whine and complain. Instead, they look within their hearts for that true passion that ignites that spark and gets them fired up for their dream.

Ultimately, you are responsible for whether or not you achieve your goals and dreams. Responsibility is the ability to respond to a situation. Your response will actually depend on what you've done to prepare yourself for that situation. Benjamin Franklin said it best, "By failing to prepare, you are preparing to fail." Preparation is the first step not the last. It gets you ready for what you may or may not encounter in life. It makes you confident in your response to adversity.

If you don't have your armor on, then how can you really expect to win the battle against fear, doubt, procrastination, naysayers, etc.? You simply can't do it. So, what do you do to prepare? Get emotional about your dream by saying your affirmations out loud everyday, develop a mastermind team of positive people that believe in you, immerse yourself in personal development material and build a dream board so that you can visualize yourself achieving your dreams. There are many other things that you can do to prepare, but these are the basics that will develop your foundation and prepare you for battle.

You have to make a decision today to get committed to the emotions inside of your heart that will become the driving force behind your ability to achieve your goals and dreams. If those emotions have been lying dormant for years, because someone stole your dream, then it's time to wake them up and start believing in yourself again. Remember, I believe in you and I won't allow you to quit on me or yourself. I know you can do it! I believe you can do it! My belief in you probably stirred up some emotions in your heart. If so, let those emotions motivate you to go for your dreams!

Who are the people that you hang out with on a daily basis? Are they motivators? Are they people that you admire? **OR** Are they losers? Are they people whose only enjoyment comes from arriving home from their J.O.B. and watching television? According to the A.C. Nielsen Co., the average American watches more than four hours of television each day. That's twenty-eight hours per week, or two months of nonstop TV-watching per year. In a sixty-five year life, that person will have spent nine years glued to the tube. That same person will moan and complain about their life, but did absolutely nothing to change it. Does this sound like some of your friends? If so, it's time for you to make some decisions about your associations.

Proverbs 11:14 says "Where no wise guidance is, the people fall, but in the multitude of counselors there is safety." You have to surround yourself with people that provide you with wisdom and guidance. Make a decision today to build a mastermind team of positive people that believe in you and your dreams.

Your physical fitness and social network are just two areas of your life that you make daily decisions about that shape the rest of your life. What about the other areas? What decisions are you making today that will predict your future?

Question #2 - What's your Why in life? Your Why is your ultimate purpose in life. It's the very reason that you get out of bed every single day. I have a very powerful Why that keeps me laser-focused on the road of success and prosperity. I speak my Why out loud on a daily basis, not just once, but many times. Speaking your Why helps to move it into existence. The power of the spoken word is unimaginable. Its power is incomprehensible.

Dr. Creflo Dollar is one of my greatest spiritual mentors. I was recently reviewing one of his online Bible studies and found this statement about words:

> "The power to change begins with your words. Your words have serious power; and good or bad, you will have what you say. When you begin to take responsibility for your words, you will change your life. Judge your speech and train yourself to only speak what you believe. By speaking faith-filled words, you position yourself to receive the promises of God."

As usual, Creflo over-delivered by providing this Bible reference to back up what he had said:

> Proverbs 18: 20-21 says "A man shall be filled with the fruit of his words whether good or evil. Death and life are in the power of the tongue.

I want you to take a minute to really internalize what Dr. Dollar emphasized in this teaching. It's important that you understand the words that you speak shape your life – good or bad. I challenge you to stop allowing negative words to curse your life and start speaking blessings over yourself and your family everyday by saying your Why out loud for the world to hear.

I know some of you reading this may being saying, "But John…How can I say my Why out loud if I have no idea what it is?" Your Why is what naturally drives you and creates your daily decisions and actions. If you don't know your Why yet, don't worry. Take some time to really examine this question and to think about WHY you're here on this beautiful planet Earth. God has a purpose for everyone. Get quiet, turn within, and search for the answer. Grab a piece of paper and just starting writing your Why in life. It will flow effortlessly once you start. Most importantly, make sure your Why is truly yours and not the Why of someone else. Don't ask anyone their opinion about your Why. It has to be yours! You only have one life so take action and decide what you ultimately want to do with it.

Growing up, labels were placed on all of us. Family, friends, schoolmates, and society in general had their own ideas of what we should be doing with our lives. However, they rarely took the time to shape their own lives. Instead, they lived vicariously through you. Have you been living their Why, the life they think you should be living? No one has the power or right to live your life except you! If you've been living someone else's life, least of all your own, begin to take control of your life and find your Why by continuing on with this chapter and asking yourself the next question.

Question #3 - Do you dream BIG? Do you allow yourself to dream big, or are you too afraid to have big, powerful dreams? Do you start to dream big but then shrink away at the fear of HOW you're going to accomplish that goal, that dream, that desire?

When you allow yourself to dream big dreams, it requires you to stretch yourself outside of your comfort zone. If you dream within your comfort zone, you are limiting yourself and your potential. What's comfortable and normal for you may be scary and difficult for me. We're all different. We all have our own dreams. ALLOW yourself to dream! Sometimes our dream muscle gets sore, small, and tired from lack of use, but it's like any other muscle in our body. If we stretch it and develop it every day, it will get stronger and more powerful day by day.

Do you know what you want for yourself in the next year, the next five years, or even the next ten years? If you don't, is it because you've stopped allowing yourself to dream? Or, have you gotten so caught up in life's daily distractions that you've stopped actively controlling and directing your future? Take action now and stop allowing life's distractions to determine your level of success. It all begins with focusing on your dreams and what you really want out of life.

I want you to come up with twenty-one dreams to reach for and achieve in the next five years. Why? Not only because of the things that you will acquire, but most importantly, because of the person you will become in the process. I guarantee you that you won't be the same person in five years as you are now IF you actively pursue those twenty-one dreams. Once you achieve even one of those dreams, you'll have gained skills and knowledge that will allow you to dream bigger and achieve even more.

Create a dream board. Gather pictures of the things you want to accomplish in the next month, year, five years, ten years, and so on. The time frame doesn't matter, but rather, it's the dreams themselves that are important. Surround yourself with these images of your dreams. Flood your subconscious with them. Allow yourself to believe in your dreams. Allow yourself to believe in yourself, in your potential, in your God-given abilities. DREAM BIG! You are more powerful than you could ever imagine.

Question #4 - Can you hear your heart's words and desires? Can you hear what your heart is saying? Can you hear what it's asking you to do? Are you on the right path that will lead you towards your heart's wishes? If you don't know the answer to these questions, you

MUST get quiet. Actively take some time, get quiet, and look within. Allow yourself to really examine these questions that I'm asking you. What is your heart saying? Is your heart full of joy or is your heart filled with the sadness, pain, and regret of living an unfulfilled life? It's NOT too late! You can take back the life that you've always wanted to live! I believe in you, maybe even more than you believe in yourself.

I want you to look past any hurt, pain, and fear you may feel, and actively begin to create and manifest your heart's desires. I promise you that those desires wouldn't be there if you couldn't achieve them. You are more powerful than you could ever imagine. The Almighty God created you, and God does not make junk! He wants you to be happy. He wants you to dream big and achieve your goals and dreams. I want this for you too. I'm here to help you create the life you've only dared to imagine.

Your heart's desire is worth more than all of the gold and money in the world. You simply can't buy the feeling that you get when you have accomplished even a little part of your life's dream. That feeling will take you through any challenge, tribulation, and storm that comes your way. It will drive you to keep striving for what you really want out of life.

Take the time to constantly thank God for instilling that little spark inside of your heart. He gave it to you, and only you, for a reason. Now, it's time for you to pour some motivational fuel on that spark to turn it into a raging fire that drives you toward the achievement of your goals and dreams. The enemy will try to extinguish your fire by casting doubt into your mind. When this happens, you refuel your fire by speaking your Why out loud in the face of the enemy. It's similar to this scene in *Rocky 2*:

> Rocky was beaten and battered by the enemy (his competitor) in the boxing ring. The announcer says "What is keeping him up, I don't know. He can't even get his gloves up to defend himself." Rocky falls again. Mick, Rocky's trainer, tells him "DOWN, DOWN, STAY DOWN!" At that moment, Rocky sees his wife, Adrianne, and gets back up for more. As he sat in the corner prepared to fight the battle of his life, he said "I ain't going down no more!" Rocky was declared the Heavyweight Champion of the World.

The enemy tried to smother Rocky's fire inside of his heart. Even his trainer was telling him that it was over. It wasn't until Rocky saw his wife and thought of his family that the little flickering spark in his heart was reignited into an inferno that lead to the achievement of his ultimate goal in life. Don't let the enemy snuff out the flame of faith in your heart. Instead, fuel that little spark with your affirmations, your dream board and your Why in life. That tiny little flicker will turn into a beautiful firestorm that will give you the strength to forge forward towards the achievement of your goals, dreams and desires.

Question #5 - What would you do if you KNEW success was guaranteed? What risks would you take if you knew you that you couldn't fail? If your success was certain, what would you do? Think about that for a second. I want you to visualize what action steps you would take if failure wasn't an option.

Unfortunately, success is not guaranteed no matter who you are or what you do. You have to step out in faith whenever you begin something new or learn about an opportunity that you know will change your life. I hear so many people say that they don't believe in faith, because they can't see it, feel it or touch it. My simple response to that is "You can't see, feel or touch gravity but you sure won't jump off a building to test it. Instead, you believe that gravity exists and you don't question it." In order to be successful, you must have the same belief about faith – you don't question it and just know in your heart that it exists. Remember, faith stands for **F**ind **A**nswers **I**n **T**he **H**eart.

I understand the frustration that most of you feel when I say that you just have to step out in faith. No, it's not comfortable. Yes, there's risk involved. But think about remaining in the same place that you are currently in and never moving forward, because you didn't have the belief in yourself to take a leap of faith that would have changed your life. What's holding you back? Is it fear? Is it uncertainty? Or is it just a matter of not making a DECISION to change your life for the better, to be the person you DESERVE to be, to use your God-given talents to influence everyone around you for the better?

Sarah Reinertsen was born different. Her left leg was deformed with a condition called proximal femoral focal deficiency (PFFD). After maneuvering on a stiff leg brace from eleven months to seven years old, the decision was made to amputate her leg. In school, Sarah was always picked last for team sports and wasn't encouraged by her coaches or teachers to engage in regular play with the other children. At the age of eleven, Sarah went to her first track meet for kids with disabilities. She finished first in the one hundred meter race. Flip forward to October 15, 2005. This was the day that Sarah finished the hardest Ironman triathlon in Kona, Hawaii in fifteen hours and five minutes. If Sarah wouldn't have taken that step of faith to go after what she wanted or allowed her disability to limit her or if she would have listened to all of the naysayers, it would be IMPOSSIBLE for her to achieve her dreams.

Who are you listening to? Are you listening to motivated teachers, reading books by inspirational authors, and attending life-changing seminars and events? Or are you choosing to listen to your loser friends, your idiot coworkers, your negative relatives, etc.? Are you surrounded by successful or mediocre people? Do they support your dreams? Do they believe in you? More importantly, do YOU believe in YOURSELF? You are the most important person in your life. Without you, the world as you know it would cease to exist. You must be the most important person in your life, because you are when it comes to determining your level of success or failure.

Stop living in fear and uncertainty. Start living a life of prosperity and abundance. Step out into the unknown and trust yourself. You will be completely supported by your faith and nothing else. I'm not sure who wrote this quote, but it pretty much sums it up in only a few words - "Faith is not belief without proof, but trust without reservation." You must believe deeply in your heart that faith exists and trust that belief without question. Your heart will lead you in the right direction IF you take that first step of faith towards your destiny.

Ask yourself this question again, "What actions would I take if I knew that success was guaranteed?" I'm sure that you could think of a whole list of actions that you would start taking today. Don't wait any longer to take those actions. Start going for your dreams now! Act as if your success is guaranteed by stepping out in faith, and you will be met with more success and prosperity than you could ever imagine.

Side note...Make sure you are asking yourself these questions in order. Don't jump forward to the next one or skip any. Each question naturally leads to the next. If you find yourself avoiding a particular question, that is the question that you need more than any other.

Question #6 - Do you immerse yourself in life-changing, inspirational and motivational material? Or do you watch waste-of-time television shows and read trashy novels? We were given four inputs (eyes & ears) and one output (mouth). Our bodies are readily equipped to immerse our minds in material that we hear and see. However, you must actively choose what you allow into your mind. Have you ever heard the saying "Garbage in, garbage out?" Whatever you listen to, read about or watch – good or bad - will pour out of your mouth like an open fire hydrant.

Everyone is a student of life in something. I continually invest in personal development materials, because I am fully invested in my future. Every single day, I listen to two hours of personal development material, because I know that the material I listen to has a direct effect on my future. Listening to motivational material helps me to stay focused and reach my heart's desires. I am actively committed to achieving my goals and dreams. By listening to motivational material and attending life-changing personal development seminars, I am surrounded by people that support me along my pursuit of success. I am continually surrounded by teachings, people, and information that focus on allowing me to dream big, believe in myself, and achieve all that I could ever imagine!

How are you spending your time? What are you actively choosing to listen to? What noises and words are your ears being exposed to? The choice is YOURS for the making. Most of you reading this are likely saying "John, I just don't have two hours every day to devote to motivational materials." Believe me when I say that I understand busy schedules, and I recommend that you start small. Just 1/96th of your day is enough to get you started.

Let me explain. 1/96th of twenty-four hours is fifteen minutes. Just fifteen minutes a day is all it takes for you to begin to see your results EXPLODE! Invest in some type of personal development CD, DVD or book. Not just anything…something that you know will assist you along your success journey. Most likely, you have something already sitting around that has become shelf-help instead of self-help. Start today by picking it up and devoting fifteen minutes a day to that material until you finish it. I also recommend that you journal what you learn from each fifteen minute segment. Of course, you can invest more time, but the 1/96th of a day habit is a great way to start.

Allow the motivational, inspirational material to get inside your heart. When you allow the words of positive motivation to get inside your heart and create a solid, rock hard foundation, you will truly begin to live the life of your dreams! Your desire to listen to naysayers, gossip, negative TV programs, etc. will sharply decline, because you begin to realize that those things are only hindering your success.

Question #7 - Are you completely passionate about your ultimate Why in life? Most people start out with bigger than life dreams, and the passion underlying their dreams is fire hot. Over time, they continually water down their dreams and goals to fit their current surrounds or situations in life and that passion slowly disappears.

If you leave a plant out in the sun and forget to water it, what happens? Of course, without water the plant will die, because the seed isn't receiving the nourishment that it needs to grow. Similarly, your passion for your dreams must be continually fed. If you just let it sit in the back of your mind, then it will slowly die just like the plant.

This is SO important! You can't just leave your dream lying around to fend for itself. You must feed it every day by releasing the passion in your heart that originally got you fired up about your dream and made you believe that it was even possible. This is the nourishment that will keep your dream alive. After all, if you don't have the desire to achieve something, then likely you won't.

Keeping your passion strong is not easy. It will require you to invest time in saying your affirmations, reading and/or listening to personal development material, building a dream wall and associating with people (a mastermind team) that believes in your dream as much as you do.

Don't shy away from the bad days when you simply can't fathom the possibility that you will ever achieve your dream. On the journey of success, bad days are bound to occur. When it happens, just allow yourself to be stretched outside of your comfort zone into believing that you can do it. You will NEVER stretch, NEVER grow, and NEVER achieve success unless you are willing to pay the price during these bad days.

Nancilea Foster began diving when she was only five years old. Her passion for the sport kept her committed to the long hours of rigorous training. At the age of fourteen, her dreams were nearly shattered when her head slammed against the board during a routine dive. The accident broke her jaw, knocked out nine teeth, shattered cheek and sinus bones and caved in part of her nose. Despite her injuries and fear, Nacilea's passion for the sport led her back to the diving board.

Eight months later, it happened again. Most people would have given up after the first accident. After recovering from the second set of injuries, Nancilea headed back to the diving board. She struggled with fear, but her ultimate passion, her faith in Christ, gave her the strength to keep going. Nancilea's willingness to pay the price for her dream led her to the 2008 Beijing Olympics, where she placed eighth in the 3-meter springboard final.

Can you even imagine how easy it would have been for Nancilea to give up after her first accident? Hearing stories about champions like Nancilea makes most of us realize that your worst day on your success journey could never compare with what she faced not once, but twice. She battled the fear and doubt that often cause people to quit. Nancilea's passion for life and her dream conquered her biggest nightmare.

Do you have that kind of passion for your dream? If not, then you haven't found your ultimate purpose in life yet. You will know it when you discover it, because your passion for it will almost overwhelm you. Just like Nancilea, you must let the passion drive you and be willing to pay the price for your dream no matter what adversity you may face.

Question #8 - Will you step up and live the champion life? The word "champion" has been defined as a fighter or a warrior. Another definition is someone that fights for a person or a cause. As you relentlessly pursue your ultimate dream in life, you must take a champion stance and fight for your dream. I'm not talking about a physical confrontation. However, you must be just as ferocious in your fight for your dreams. Realize that the enemy has placed adversity in your life to stop you and you simply can't let it happen because you are a champion!

When you commit to living the champion life, you talk, walk, believe, dream, build, stretch, motivate, and fly like a champion. Are you living like a champion now? Do you associate with other champions? Whether or not other people see you as a champion isn't important. What's crucially important is that you see yourself as the champion you were born to be!

We're all born champions, each and every one of us. Sometimes, we just forget that simple fact so tell yourself each and every day:

I am a champion!
I am dreaming like a champion!
I am walking like a champion!
I am challenging myself like a champion!

Champions make decisions. Champions know their Why. Champions dream huge. Champions listen to and hear their heart's desires. Champions act as if their success is guaranteed. Champions listen to motivational materials. Champions step up and live the champion life!

If you successfully completed this chapter by asking yourself all eight questions and answering them honestly, then you are a champion.

You made a decision to invest in your future. You, my friend, are well on your way to achieving ultimate success!

Principle V
Insure Your Dream

Without insurance, your dream is dead. Let me say it again. Without insurance, your dream is dead! We have home insurance, health insurance, car insurance, life insurance, all kinds of insurance to protect our "stuff." Unfortunately, most of us treat our stuff better than we treat our dream – our very reason for living. That's why 97% of people in the world are dead broke by the age of sixty-five and only 3% are successful.

Do you have dream insurance? You must have a rock solid plan in place to protect your goal and dreams before you can ever stand face to face with the enemy. For example, if someone challenges your ability to achieve your dream, what do you do? If you begin to stammer over your words and don't have foundational belief in yourself, then that person will steal your dream. When you have dream insurance, your success is indestructible.

I'm going to breakdown the word "insurance" for you and lay out a plan of action to protect your dream. If you physically take the time to prepare for a hurricane, then your house and belongings will be protected. Similarly, if you take the time to lay out a plan to protect your dream and make the decision to be in that top 3%, then your success is inevitable!

I - For 97% of the world's population, "I" stands for indecision. They can't make a decision. Go to any restaurant and you'll see this for yourself. When asked if they ready to order, nearly every answer will be - "No, I don't know what I want. Go on to the next person." They've had several minutes to make a decision about something as simple as what to eat, and they still can't decide! What do you think happens when they're faced with a real, life-changing decision? Nothing! They're paralyzed by fear. They're afraid of making a mistake. They ask other indecisive people around them what they should do.

Inside the word indecision is decision. Make a decision right now to develop and live free from the nonsense of the world. Associate with other champions. Never ever give up in the pursuit of your dreams. Keep progressing towards the achievement of your goals and dreams and remain confident in your decision. The moment that you give up and listen to the enemy, you've quit. You've given up on your dream. You must never give up on your dream! God birthed that dream inside of you so that you could realize it and see its fulfillment. It's no mistake that you have big dreams for your life. Do yourself and the world a favor; follow your passion. Follow what drives you forward. You owe it to yourself, to others, and to God.

While 97% of people are indecisive, 3% of people are inspired. Champions are inspired by their dream and their purpose. They are continually inspired and fulfilled and inadvertently inspire other people around them. Inspiration radiates from them, because they believe in themselves and their dreams with every ounce of their being.

When you're inspired, you take action. You see your dream, your vision, your goal, and you move towards it. Action is one of the most important factors in achieving success. You can visualize and say affirmations all you want, but if you don't take strategic action towards the achievement of your goals and dreams, nothing is going to change. You simply can't attract success, you have to take aggressive action to achieve it.

One of the best action steps that you can take to propel yourself towards your goals and dreams is to examine what you fear. Is there something that you fear so much that is getting in the way of your dream? Maybe it's prospecting. Maybe it's changing your diet. Maybe it's getting away from your negative associations. Without reading any further, I want you to think of the thing that you fear the most that is preventing you from achieving your dreams. After you have a clear image in your mind of that fear, I want you to commit to overcoming it. How? By just doing it.

You will be absolutely amazed how quickly your life will begin to change if you simply just do the things you fear. The sooner you face them, the better! After you conquer your greatest fear, every other obstacle in your success path will become easier to overcome. Here's a great acronym to assist you in overcoming your FEAR:

F – Face it and don't back down.

E – Extinguish it. Commit to no longer letting fear stop you.

A – Annihilate it. The fear is gone forever!

R – Return to your dream. Keep forging forward towards success.

Once again…just do it! Get inspired to take the action needed to finally achieve the things in life that you've only dreamed of until now.

N – This letter stands for negative. Unfortunately, most people, 97% of them, in this world are negative. They focus on what's not working in their lives and the lives of everyone else around them. These people spend their time reading the newspaper, complaining about the weather, watching the news, etc. If you saturate yourself with negativity long enough, you become negative. If you hang around negative people long enough, you become negative. It's not rocket science. Negative in equals negative out.

Yes, we all have our moments. It's impossible not to have a negative thought cross your mind ever in your life. However, most people take it to the extreme. They refuse to see what's good and positive in their lives. They're not willing to take active control over their destiny. Champion, you're either going forward towards your dream or backwards to listen to and associate with the negative naysayers. There's no other way to go. Which path you choose is entirely up to you. I can't decide for you. If you are tired of all the negativity, then take make the decision to get it out of your life forever.

I said that "N" stands for the negative 97% crowd. However, "N" also stands for a word that describes the 3%'ers - notorious. They are recognized for their ambition and determination. I was notorious in changing my own life as a clinically diagnosed stutterer. Everyone saw me as a stutterer and believed that I was a stutterer. But I refused to see myself as a stutterer. I read and listened a lot. I learned how to see the possible inside the impossible. I learned how to see my ability inside of my disability. I began speaking my future into existence. I became notorious to my family and friends for my crazy idea that I could actually overcome my stuttering disability.

I didn't let their opinions stop me from becoming an international, motivational speaker. My God-given destiny is to change peoples' lives through my teachings, and I wasn't about to let anyone tell me that I couldn't do it. I am notorious for speaking my mind to anyone that challenges me or tries to hold me back from fulfilling my destiny of empowering and motivating champions around the world.

What are you notorious for? Do you believe you were put on this Earth to change peoples' lives? I believe that you were. If people try to get in your way and stop you on your journey to success and prosperity, tell them to step aside or climb aboard. It's as simple as that. Get out of my way or come with me. Join the 3% crowd and be known by everyone as the notorious dreamer that won't let anyone or anything stop you from your God-given destiny.

S – Basically, "S" represents the "**S**ee What Happens" people in the 97% crowd. We've all encountered them. They don't plan out their days. They don't take control of their lives. They've never set a goal before, and if they did, they gave up on it at the first sign of adversity. Instead, they just sit back and see what happens. That's their answer for everything, "I'll just see what happens." The results in their life are basically dependent on everything and everyone else in the world except for them. That's no way to live your life!

A great example of this mentality deals with people that read horoscopes. "Well, my horoscope has been telling me for the last six months that I'd be experiencing some challenges and setbacks. John, I just can't move forward because it says so in the alignment of the planets. There's nothing I can do!" Excuse my language, but that is such a bunch of crap.

You know what a horoscope is? It's a horror scope. Yes, a HORROR SCOPE! I have personally coached people that use their horror scopes to explain why they can't gain active control over their lives. It's an excuse not a reality! They're using their horror scope as justification for not living the life they want to live. Being a passive bystander in your own life will never lead to the achievement of your goals and dreams. You might as well be living someone else's life. Well, actually, you are, if you're allowing your life to be completely controlled by outside influences.

You know what's better than a horror scope? How about developing a vision scope? A vision scope is the best kind of scope out there. When you look through your vision scope, you are able to look forward. You don't look back at the past. You don't let your present results dictate where you're headed. You decide what you want and choose to stay focused on your vision. Doesn't that make a lot more sense than using a horror scope? It's your life, why not make the most of it?

Lose the "See What Happens" mentality. Join the 3% crowd and develop the Stickability attitude. Yes, that's another "S" word for you. Actually, it's a word that I completely made up that basically means that you must be persistent in pursuit of your goal and stick to it. Have you ever gotten a piece of gum on something? It's nearly impossible to remove it. That's how you have to be with your dream. Stick to it and be resistant to anything or anyone that tries to remove your belief in it. Your vision scope combined with stickability will guarantee your success!

The great Les Brown once said "Whatever is impossible is possible, for the impossible can be achieved." When I heard that statement, it changed my life. It reconfirmed for me my decision to stick to following my heart's desires. Everything in this world has a polar opposite. If something is impossible, it must also be possible. It wouldn't be able to exist otherwise.

I was willing to be stuck....completely glued to my dream of becoming a fluent speaker. My family and friends told me I was losing my mind, because I wasn't listening to what anybody said. They were right! I was losing the mind of a clinically diagnosed stutterer and gaining the mind of a champion. I refused to listen to the enemy even when they were right in my face. I stayed focused on my vision of being a great communicator and retiring to South Florida by the age of 30. Due to my vision and my stickability, I moved to South Florida at 29 years, 11 months, and 18 days of age as a millionaire speaker!

Your dream has more power hidden inside of it than you could even imagine. Things you could never even comprehend will occur when you remain focused and dedicated to your dream. You must be committed to your journey regardless of what anyone else says. Your dream really is that important. It's YOUR dream. They can't see it, but you can! If you can see it, you can achieve it! They can't achieve it because they don't see it, at least not yet. But when you achieve that goal, that's when they'll believe you. It's not their fault. They just couldn't see what you could see. You could explain it to them a million times, and they still probably wouldn't see it.

    U – This letter stands for **U**nder-deliver. 97% of people work at their J.O.B. (Just Over Broke), because they have to, not because that's what they love to do. They go into work late and leave early. They take a long lunch, and always manage to squeeze in their two fifteen minute breaks that they are owed by their employer. They do just enough to ensure their job stability. They do just what's required of them, not only in their job, but in every area of their life. They do just enough to get by. They never break out of the mold of their daily routine. They never take a chance or try anything new. They UNDER-DELIVER!

    How many people do you know that live like that? A lot, right? I do. Have you ever tried telling them your goal? Have you ever told them, "I know what I want and I know where I'm going. I don't know how I'm going to get there or how I'm going to do it, but I'm staying committed to what I want, and I'm going for it!" They probably looked at you as though you were nuts, right? They thought, "Who are you to change your life? Only the lucky are able to do that, and you're not one of them!"

NEVER listen to the doubters! That's what they are. They doubt everything in their own lives and everyone else's lives as well. They were born a champion with the right to achieve greatness, but they allowed society to mold them into someone that does just enough to get by in life. They don't know any better. But just because they don't know any better, that doesn't mean you should listen to them.

If you share your goal and where you're headed with someone, and they look at you as though you're a nutcase, use that as fuel to drive you forward. They're in that 97% crowd, and you're in the 3% crowd. No, I'm not saying that you are better than them. You have simply made better decisions than they have in your life. Stay focused on being a 3%'er when you begin to doubt yourself and your dream.

I hate to break this to you but...You must be abnormal in the pursuit of your dreams. Abnormal means you are above normal. You're above the norm. You're so dedicated to your dreams that you go above and beyond the call of duty. You do more than what is expected of you, because you know that it's an investment in your future. You continually over-deliver, because you know it's an investment in your dream and in your future.

By only doing the bare minimum, you never grow. Your dream will actually start to die and decay if you don't continually grow and stretch yourself. As a 3%'er, you are **U**nbelievable instead of an Under-

Deliverer. You do things that sound completely unbelievable to others. When people say "Come on, you can't do that!", do it anyway. Do not listen to the people that chronically under-deliver! They wouldn't know a dream if it hit them in the face. They only see the believable. They can't see their own vision, let alone yours. If you listen to them and stop moving towards your dream, you become a 97%'er. It's completely irresponsible for you to allow that to happen.

Most people simply can't see your dream. Why is that? Because they aren't used to looking outside of the box. They don't know what it's like to have a dream, a vision, a goal. They let outside circumstances stop them from living the life that they want to live. The most important thing is that YOU can see your dream. You are able to look past adversities and circumstances and see the future. You understand that only you can create the future that you desire. You can let outside people positively influence your decisions on your future, but you and you alone create it.

The 3%'ers do the unbelievable, because they know it will bring them one step closer to their dream. They know that those actions will create immense amounts of momentum towards their goal. They continually step outside of their comfort zone and do things that seem impossible or scary. When you step outside of your comfort zone and do things that seem unbelievable or incomprehensible, amazing things begin to happen. God wants you to step out in faith and create the unimaginable. Inside unimaginable is imaginable, and inside imaginable is an "able image." Once you see it in your imagination, you're able to carry it out. You're able to move towards it.

Your image, your dream, is worth more than all of the gold in the world. You either go for the gold or go home. There's no other way to go! Are you going to willingly give it away in the face of your enemy? I'll say it again. Are you going to relinquish your dream in the face of your enemy? Your enemy doesn't believe in the impossible or unimaginable. They never learned how to look beyond the surface and see what's hidden just beyond the mind's eye. If you listen to them, you've given up on the unbelievable. When your enemy says, "Who do you think you are," respond by saying, "I'm unbelievable. I'm abnormal. I'm an action-taking champion in pursuit of my dreams." It is so important for you to truly believe that and live by these statements.

R - 97% of people are stuck in a **R**ut. Their typical response to "What's going on?" is "Nothing." Where are they going with that attitude? Nowhere! They're too stuck in their rut to move to the next level. They've settled for what's comfortable, which means that they've settled for how things are and have no motivation to change.

I love when I hear people talking to their friends and they say "What's going on?" The friend responds "Nothing. Come on over." Let me give you a clue... Don't go over there! It only makes sense. If there's nothing going on, why would you waste your time? Remember, your future is greatly determined by who you spend your time with. If you hang out with people that are stuck in a rut and going nowhere, soon you'll be in a rut, too. Do you really want to be sitting around doing nothing forever?

Champions are continually moving forward and developing new dreams, goals, and visions. They want to push and develop themselves as much as possible, because in so doing, they are an inspiration to others. When someone accomplishes the impossible, it's as though they're telling everyone else, "I did it, and you can do it too!" People that are stuck in a rut are comfortable.

Don't get comfortable. Get uncomfortable, because discomfort causes you to move. It causes you to take action. Remember, if you're not moving, you're dying. If you're not moving, you're not helping other people. You're basically saying, "I'm comfortable with what I have, I don't want anything more. Leave me alone and I'll be just fine." Mediocrity is not for you! Live your life with passion. Live your life with honor. Live your life knowing that you are making a difference and making a positive contribution to other peoples' lives.

Champion 3%'ers are **Relentless** when it comes to their dreams. They smile when the naysayers tell them "You're still going to seminars?

Come on, that stuff doesn't work. Why do you keep blowing your money on books and CDs. It's a money making scam!" You have to be relentless in pursuit of your dreams to handle comments like that. If it ever gets to you, just take a look at the status of their life. Where are they headed? Nowhere! What are they doing? Nothing! You can't let people like that distract you from your calling.

What happens when you don't read or listen to motivational material for five days? Your brain starts to get dirty. We're surrounded by negativity. You start to listen to the people around you. "Maybe they're right. Maybe my dream really is too unbelievable." You must be relentless and focus on your dream every single day. The famous motivational speaker Zig Ziglar says, "Some people say motivation doesn't last. Neither does a shower. That's why you do it every day."

You have to immerse yourself in personal development on a daily basis so that the negativity doesn't cause you to lose focus. You don't take a shower once and expect it to last ten years. You don't eat once and expect not to get hungry again for a week. So, why would you think reading one book in five years is going to help you achieve your dreams? It sounds ridiculous because it is! Be relentless and refuse to be stuck in a rut.

A - This letter represents what everyone does at one point or another - **A**nalyze everything. However, 97% people typically don't just analyze something. They overanalyze it to prevent themselves from making a decision. "Should I invest in that seminar? I don't know. Do I have enough time? How much does it cost? Can I get a refund? What will my friends think?" Then instead of actually considering how this one thing might actually change their life, they ask their negative friends and family members what they should do. Of course, they say "NO!" They're analyzers too. Analyzers look at all of the facts and details before they make a decision. They take their eye off of their vision for the future. They stop focusing on the possible or believable and instead focus on the practical and realistic.

If you ask someone for their opinion about your goals and dreams, they won't hesitate to tell you what they think. They'll say, "You're crazy. Who are you to think you can achieve that?" They don't know who you are. How could they? Remember, you're developing an insurance plan to protect your dreams so you can't waste a moment worrying about what they say. You don't want losers in your insurance plan, do you? I don't see why you would. There is no reason for them to be involved in the process of achieving your dream. They will only hold you back! Only allow people that believe in you and your dream to be involved in your insurance plan.

One of my most favorite things to do that just happens to begin with "A" is **A**nnihilating the enemy. To be in the 3% crowd, you must be relentless in pursuit of dreams and annihilate the disbelievers and dream stealers that get in your way. No, I don't mean physically annihilate them. Just stop associating with them and refuse to let their negativity impact your life. You can also take an offensive approach to annihilating the enemy of your dreams. All you need to do is a little bit more than you've been doing. Take a look at what everyone else is doing and do the opposite. Do something that seems impractical or improbable. It will skyrocket your success, and your focus will cause the enemy to run the other way.

Geniuses are the type of people that do everything outside of the norm and live life completely differently than anyone else. Why? Because they allow themselves to see what no one else sees, believe what no one else believes, and are willing to step out in faith to achieve the unrealistic expectation that they have. Albert Einstein saw what no one else was able to see. Genius – yes. Perfect – no. Many people don't know that Einstein had a speech challenge as a child, and he actually failed his school entrance exam. After graduating with an average school record, Einstein had problems finding a job and even questioned his decision to become a physicist. As you see, Einstein wasn't a perfect being but he was able to achieve his goals, because he believed that he could and he believed in himself.

When his theories about science and the way the universe works were proven to be correct, he gained the utmost respect not only from other scientists, but from people all over the world. Einstein truly was a genius in his field of study and lived outside of the norm to achieve greatness. As one of the most intellectual men in the world, even he had his challenges.

You don't have to be a genius to discover something new, something incredible, or something revolutionary. It happens everyday by people just like you that simply followed their dreams and believed in something that only they could see. Let me ask you a question...Can you see your dream coming true? If not, then there's no way that you will achieve it. Before you can accomplish anything in life, you have to believe with all of your heart that it is possible.

Let me take this time to tell you about another million dollar tool that will help you annihilate the enemy of fear and skyrocket your level of belief. This simple yet life-changing device is called a pillow speaker. When you're sleeping, attached the pillow speaker to your mp3 player, set your player to repeat your favorite motivational teachings and tuck it underneath your pillow. As you listen to this material, your mind will be infused with positive motivational messages. It shouldn't be so loud that it disturbs your sleep. This doesn't take the place of your daily personal self-development. It's just that little bit of extra that will create extraordinary results.

N – This letter stands for Nothing. Why? Because that's what 97% of people have going on in their lives...NOTHING! Remember, you want to stay away from these people. How exciting is nothing? Not exciting in the least! If nothing is going on, THEN you're living a dull and meaningless existence. You're refusing to see the blessings that surround you. Every single person has an infinite amount of blessings in their lives, but sadly most people never see them.

For the 3% crowd, the letter "N" stands for "Nothing will stop me." Even if you don't know how you're going to achieve your goal, as long as you know why you are doing what you are doing and you believe in yourself and your dream, that's enough. Most successful people didn't know how they were going to achieve their goal when they first set it. But they kept going nonetheless, because they believed in their dream enough to know that nothing would stop them from achieving it.

Henry Ford dreamed of producing an automobile that was reasonably priced, reliable, and efficient. Most importantly, he wanted the automobile to be affordable to ordinary people and not just the wealthy. He became laser-focused on his product and customer base to achieve his dream. Several major financial backers actually left Ford, because he refused to introduce a car that he didn't feel was ready for customers. There were also many people that questioned his abilities, and his right to even legally manufacture automobiles. But that didn't stop him.

In October 1908 when announcing the birth of the Model T, Ford proclaimed "I will build a motor car for the great multitude." Because of Ford's dream, the Model T automobile was one of the greatest changes in the lives of common people in history. Can you imagine how much different the world would be if Henry Ford had listened to everyone around him? Thank God Henry Ford believed in his vision and was relentless in pursuit of his dream.

How often do you let what someone else said or another obstacle keep you from achieving your dream? Are you as relentless and persistent as Ford? If not, what's stopping you? Move beyond your fear and self-doubt and allow absolutely nothing to stand in the way of your success.

C - For the 97% of people, **C** stands for **Casual**. Most people are casual about their life. You could even call them passive observers. They let life pass them by day after day. Casual people are bored in life. They don't know that life can be absolutely amazing if they only made a decision to dream big and step outside the societal role that they have conformed to over the years.

Casual is synonymous with comfortable. Casual clothing is seen and defined as simple and comfortable. You already know how I feel about being comfortable. When you're comfortable, you're not growing! You're settling for things as they are at that very moment in life.

Even billionaires are constantly growing and expanding. It wasn't enough for Bill Gates to create Microsoft and become a multi-billionaire. He didn't want to stop there. Now he runs the Bill and Melinda Gates Foundation, one of the largest funded non-profit organizations in the world. Could he have stopped and settled for being the chief officer of Microsoft? Sure he could have! But he knows how important it is to keep pushing yourself and keep developing new dreams and visions. He's dedicated to helping the world in more ways than one and knows that being comfortable does not contribute to society in a positive way.

Are you casual in regards to your life? Do you let your dreams go by unnoticed because you think those dreams are bigger than you? Let me tell you something champion, you are so much bigger than your dreams. If you weren't, you wouldn't even have the mental capability to think them up. As the famed author of *Think and Grow Rich,* Napoleon Hill said, "What the mind can conceive, it can achieve." I believe these words with all of my heart.

Those in the 3% group believe in staying **C**ommitted. You must be absolutely committed to your dream. If you're not, no one else will be. No one else will believe in your dream if you don't. You must be so committed to your dream that you can see it, taste it, touch it, feel it, and smell it. Your vision can become your reality if you're committed.

When you make a commitment to someone, that commitment is as good as gold. People take commitments very seriously. If you break a commitment, it's as though you don't value the other person. You will more than likely lose that person's respect. You may even lose all possibility of doing business with them again. When you give your word to someone that you are committed, they expect you to uphold your end of the bargain. When you don't, you not only disappoint them, you disappoint yourself.

Have you ever made a commitment to yourself and broken it? Perhaps you committed to exercise five days a week. Perhaps you committed to quit smoking. How did it feel when you broke that commitment? It didn't feel very good, did it? When it comes to your dream, you are the most important person in your life. When you break your own commitment, it's as though you've given up on yourself. Make a commitment to keep your commitments. Don't allow yourself to break them. Commitment will take you to places you never thought you could reach and beyond all realms of expectation.

E – Here's where 97% of people just lose it. "E" stands for Enough. "I've had enough of this. I've had enough of dreaming, quitting is much easier. This is too hard. I've simply had enough!" These people give up on their dream. They dwell on the adversity rather than focusing on their dream. They forget that their vision controls their future, and they control their vision! They've had enough of dreaming. They've had enough of thinking about how they'd like to live their life. It's so sad to think about the number of unfulfilled dreams that exist in the world.

There are an infinite number of unfulfilled dreams, because there are an infinite number of ideas that people simply give up on. But remember, everything has an opposite. If there are an infinite number of unfulfilled dreams, there are an infinite number of fulfilled dreams of people just like you that simply refused to quit.

Those people are in the 3% group and are **E**mpowered by their dream. Their dream fuels them. They gain power from it. They wake up feeling good about themselves and blessed to have the ability to achieve their dream. In the old Greek, blessed means empowered to prosper. You have to be empowered to surpass mediocrity and achieve greatness.

The amazing thing is that when you are committed to achieving your dream, you not only empower yourself, but you empower the people around you to want more out of life. Empowerment is contagious. When you're empowered, other people are empowered!

Now that you have an insurance plan for your dream, you'll be able to stand toe to toe with anyone that challenges your ability to achieve it. Remember, you have made the decision to join the 3% crowd. Don't listen to the naysayers or those stuck in the 97% group. It's your dream so protect it!

Principle VI
Make a Decision Not an Excuse

Theodore Roosevelt once said "In any moment of decision, the best thing you can do is the right thing, the next best thing is the wrong thing, and the worst thing you can do is nothing." In life, we make decisions every day. Some are so habitual that we don't really even have to make a conscious decision, we just do it. Others require a little more thought, but we usually follow through based on our better judgment. The most important decisions make us consider all factors involved and then we struggle with our final choice. It's like mental tug-of-war. As President Roosevelt pointed out, the worst thing that you can do at that point of uncertainty is nothing.

When faced with a tough decision, have you ever said "I'll have to think about it?" I know I have on several occasions. However for many people, the "thinking about it" process drags out and becomes the "I'm avoiding making a decision" phase. It's smart to weigh your options, ask the advice of colleagues and consider alternatives; however, simply not making a challenging decision is irresponsible. It's not just going to go away. It will still be there when you wake up every morning and will hang over you like a dark cloud until you take action.

What's worse is that the failure to make a decision is progressive or should I say regressive. After the "I'm avoiding making a decision" phase, you start to ease the stress of the decision by making excuses. I've heard every excuse in the book. It's really amazing what someone will say just to avoid making a decision. The worst is when the excuse is a complete lie. Not only has the action moved from an excuse to lying, but remember the words that we speak often come true so be careful what you say to get out of simply making a decision.

Instead of engaging in all that foolishness and wasting everyone's time, look at the decision as an opportunity. You have been given the power to make a significant change in the world by the choice that you make. Now, I'm not going tell you that that choice will be right 100% of the time, but how will you ever know if you don't step out in faith and take that risk. Every hard decision takes courage.

On September 19, 1999, twenty year old Jaqueline Saburido and four friends were on their way home from a birthday party when an SUV driven by a drunk driver slammed into their car. Within minutes, the car caught fire and Jacqui was pinned in the front seat. She suffered burns over 60% of her body and her chances of surviving were slim. Jacqui lived, but her injuries were devastating.

She lost her hair, ears, nose and her hands were so badly burned that all of her fingers had to be amputated. Her left eyelid was removed and most of her vision is gone. Jacqui has had more than fifty operations since the crash and has many more to go. It would have been easy for Jacqui to give up at any point, but she made the courageous decision to keep living her life. Jacqui continues to tell her story worldwide and speaks out against drunk driving in national campaigns.

What if she had made the decision to give up? It would have been so easy for Jacqui to lock herself away from the world forever and use every excuse available not to continue her fight. No one would have blamed her if she did. During an interview, Jacqui said "If you want to do anything, never give up. You need to keep going. Continue to live. Whatever happens in your life, you need to keep going and be happy." Through her courageous decision to keep going, Jacqui has touched the lives of millions worldwide but more importantly she has saved the lives of hundreds possibly thousands as an advocate against drunk driving.

You have the chance to change lives with your decisions too. At the heart of every dream is the desire to touch the life of another person. I have many students that dream of achieving a certain level of success so that they can help other people. Ultimately, if they fail to make a decision to stay committed to that dream, then those people that they dreamed of helping will remain in the same position. Is that a harsh statement? Yes, but it's absolutely true.

One of my elite coaching clients dreamed of building one hundred orphanages in India. She had even toured the devastated areas and seen the orphan children eating out of garbage cans. Those images stuck with her as she built her business, but she was still full of excuses as to why her business wasn't growing more rapidly. It didn't take long to figure out that she wasn't implementing all of the strategies that she had learned from our coaching, and the result was a business plateau. Basically, her business wasn't declining but it wasn't growing either.

Once she figured out that SHE was actually causing her dream of building one hundred orphanages to slip away, she stopped all the excuses and made the decision to start building her business the right way. Why? Because she realized what was at risk if she didn't make the right choice. What's at risk for you? Is your failure to make decisions worth the loss of your dream?

At this moment in your dream building process, your life is in your hands. You have the ability to make a decision versus an excuse. You are either stepping out and standing up in decision land, or you are lazily sitting in excuse land. You're either achieving your dreams through making decisions, or you're waving your dreams goodbye as you're making excuses. You have the God-given ability to make a decision versus making an excuse so use it.

One of my favorite quotes is "Decision plus action equals results." You first have to make the decision and then take the needed action to create the results that you desire. This works both for us and against us.

Let me give you an example. If you make the decision that you want to lose weight and you take the action of exercising for an hour a day, then you will likely achieve the result that you desire. However, if you make the decision to lose weight and your only action is sitting on the couch all day watching television, then you will likely achieve undesirable results. Like I said, "Decision plus action equals results". It's inevitable!

Excuses are always followed by reasons of why you can't do something. "I can't build my business, because I don't feel like prospecting. I can't read this book, because I get a headache reading that much. I can't attend the seminar because I don't have time and it costs too much." When you make an excuse, you instantly plant a seed in your mind that you are incapable of doing something. This is personal self-destruction. Every excuse destroys a little bit of belief in yourself and your ability to achieve your dream.

Without self-belief, there is no motivation to succeed. That's the main reason that I spend so much time immersing myself in personal self development in the morning before I start my day. Success and motivation is the first thing I hear and see in the morning and the last thing that I allow to go into my spirit as I drift off to sleep. Why am I so disciplined? Because I know that I could never overcome the adversity that I face daily if I didn't continually reinforce my belief in myself and my dreams. More importantly, I would not be confident in the decisions that I make without that belief.

When you start to question your abilities, you further put off making the decision, which is better known as procrastination. Psychologists often cite procrastination as a mechanism for coping with the anxiety associated with starting or completing any task or decision. Now, I don't always agree with what the so-called experts say, but this is a point that I agree with 100%. It's like a breath of fresh air when you push the decision aside and stop letting it worry you for a while. However, procrastination is just a temporary fix. It's much more stressful to just let the decision hang over your head and possibly get more difficult as time goes by. Like I said before, simply not making a decision is irresponsible. Procrastination will also make you lazy. Do you really want to be known as lazy and irresponsible?

Understand that you have the right to live your dream, but you have to crawl out from under the pile of excuses that have built up and make a decision to change. Inside the word challenge is change. You have to be willing to change the way you handle challenging decisions. You can't just remain where you are forever. Remember, decision plus action equals results. Take a look at your results. Are you completely satisfied with your success level in every area of your life? Reread that question. I said "completely satisfied". I did not say comfortable or complacent. To be completely satisfied means that you have achieved every level of success that you can possibly achieve in that area of your life. Personally, I don't know anyone like that.

I'm not just talking about the amount of money that you have in the bank. I want you to really think about every area of your life – physical, social, mental and financial. If you're not happy with your results in those areas, then it's time that you make a decision about where you want to be and what you're willing to do to get there. You need to make a decision and stick with it.

Your decisions must be based upon your Why, which is your ultimate purpose in life. It is the foundation for every single decision that you make. Without a Why, a focus for your life, your decisions will be aimless and haphazard. Your life will be without direction. When you go on a road trip, you have a plan of action and most importantly directions. You don't say, "I want to get from Miami to Los Angeles in three days. I'll just keep going in a northwest direction. I'm sure I'll get there eventually." You may get there eventually, but you will waste time and resources and likely become frustrated that you simply didn't grab a map.

Do you understand what I'm trying to say? Without your Why, you are living without a destination. You are without purpose, without aim, without direction. You will be like a piece of paper that's just blowing along with the wind just going with the flow. That's fine if you have no goals and want to be a spectator in the game of life. Come on...you and I both know that's not what you want! You want to be remembered for the life that you led and the lives that you changed.

I challenge you right now to expand your Why. The stronger and bigger your Why, the more decisive you'll become in your daily actions. If your Why is weak, you will eventually lose all motivation to achieve success. If you're not emotionally connected to your Why, you will abandon your goals and dreams at the first sign of defeat. Remember, your Why in life is your foundation for every decision that you make. How can you really expect to make wise decisions if your foundation has cracks in it? You can't! Instead, stand strong on your Why in life and truly believe that the ultimate achievement of your Why is possible.

Make a commitment to get focused on making new and better decisions by believing in your Why, building your self-belief and stopping all of the excuses. Your daily actions will determine your future, and your actions are halted every time you make excuses to stop moving in the direction that leads you to your Why. Just imagine that you get in your car to go to the store. You are traveling at a good rate of speed and then you reach a stop sign. No problem...you stop. As you are about to accelerate, you see another stop sign and then another and then another. It's not long before you are stopping so much that it seems as if you are never going to reach your destination. You become frustrated and just go home. That's what happens when you make excuses too! You are no longer progressing in your daily action steps that will assist you in achieving your next level of success. Excuses take over and you take three steps back with every excuse. Before long, you are back where you started and ready to just give up.

If you haven't figured it out yet, excuses challenge me. Every time that I hear an excuse, I hear fear. Fear is much easier to deal with than an excuse. An excuse can be justified. You can create a whole long list of reasons why your excuse is valid. Let me give you an example. I remember a coaching client that was scheduled to show her business plan to a potential client. We had practiced her plan many times so I knew that she was ready. She had rescheduled the appointment several times and gave me plenty of excuses why – sick child, worked late, no transportation, blah, blah, blah. When she ran out of excuses and reasons to back up those excuses, she was faced with the real reason that she didn't follow through on her decision…FEAR.

She was so afraid that she would fail that she made up excuse after excuse to try to get out of it. I told her to stop the excuses and take charge of her life! She increased her daily affirmations and the amount of time that she invested in personal development. She rebuilt her belief in herself and faced her fear head on. Within a few weeks, she stopped making excuses, showed the plan and enrolled a new person in her business.

Fear tolerated is faith contaminated. There's simply no way that you can step out in faith to achieve your dream if you continue to allow fear to steal your belief. That's right. I said it! YOU are allowing fear to determine your level of success in life. Many people try to play the old blame game, but the only way that you can defeat fear is to stand up to it.

Think about the story of David and Goliath. You have a giant named Goliath that was believed to be over nine feet tall. Then, you have David, who was so small that his body armor kept falling off. David didn't let the size of Goliath intimidate him. Instead, he walked toward the giant and prepared for battle. Goliath laughed and taunted David. Well, we all know that it didn't work out so well in the end for Goliath. If fear is your Goliath, then it's time for you to face it and extinguish it out of your life for good. There's simply no way that you can achieve the next level of success until you conquer fear.

Fear is also your body's natural reaction to stress. The body doesn't like to be stressed. It wants to remain relaxed and doesn't want to be challenged. That's why so many people eventually give up on their dream. They're not willing to challenge their body's attempt to remain in that comfort zone. As a champion, I know that you're willing to become uncomfortable and make decisions that will ultimately change your life for the better. As your coach, I'm here to challenge you and to help you make those decisions that will move you forward towards the achievement of your goals and dreams.

Let's dig a little deeper and see how your decisions are holding you back from living the life that you've always dreamed of living. I want you to write down three most challenging areas of your life. It could be finances, relationships, physical health, etc. What areas in your life are you really unhappy with at this time? Don't go any further in this reading until you've made this list.

The one thing that we just have to get out of the way before we proceed is the realization that it's your fault. That's right. Your decisions have created problematic situations in these three areas of your life. I want you to take responsibility for your decisions that have produced these poor results. Remember, decision plus action creates results – positive or negative. Yes, it's hard to admit that you are failing in some way, because of your own decisions or failure to make decisions. Let's move on to better news.

Remember, I'm here to challenge you, and the following questions won't be easy to answer. We're going to focus on how you can move forward and learn from those decisions instead of just settling for your current life results. We will look at your Why and get decisive on building that Why. After all, your Why in life is your foundation for the decisions that you make so let's make sure that it's strong enough to withstand hurricane force excuses.

The first question that I'm going to ask you is life-changing. Do your daily actions violate your Why? When I say the word violate, what do I mean? To violate something means to go against something. If you violate a law such as not stealing, you're going to pay the price. Even if you don't suffer the consequences right away, sooner or later, you're going to pay the price for your wrongdoing. A law is put in place to protect you and benefit you. When you go against it, your own protection and benefit is compromised and put at risk.

Are your daily actions violating or empowering your Why? Take a look at what you do everyday and really think about the possibility that those daily action steps are compromising your success. The root of change lies in your daily decisions. I just cannot stress enough the vital role your daily decisions play in shaping your life. I'm not concerned right now with your outward success. Your current level of success is based on all of the decisions that you've made up to this point. We're going to rebuild your future decisions. Your future decisions need not have anything to do with your past decisions. Once you choose to go in a new direction, your decisions will automatically change as a result. Instead of looking backwards at your past, you must look forward towards your future.

Now, take a good look at those three areas of your life that you want to improve. I want you to get committed to examining them and taking responsibility for them. Here's the harsh reminder again. Where you are in your life is YOUR responsibility, and no one else's. Your life has been shaped by the decisions that you've made. Not your spouse, not your children, not your friends, and not even your enemies are at fault for the decisions that you've made throughout your life. If you don't take responsibility for the current state of these three areas of your life, you'll never be able to change them.

If you're going to get committed, it is absolutely crucial that you take responsibility for the current state of these three areas right now! If you're not willing to take responsibility for your life, then you might as well stop reading this book. Go ahead and put this book down. I say this because until you take full responsibility for your life, you will never move forward and claim the life that you want to live. Have you taken full responsibility for your life? If so, read on.

I want you to examine the three areas of your life that you want to change. Ask yourself right, "What action steps can I take today that will allow me to reshape my future? What can I do today to help move me from where my life is now to where I want my life to be?" Do you want to achieve your Why bad enough to make new decisions? Is your why worth pursuing regardless of the cost? Are you willing to face the criticism that will accompany you in your journey? Remember, when you start to change your life for the better, your enemies pop up. People begin to challenge you. You've got to be prepared for those challenges that people will present you with. If you've already met those enemies and you're still moving forward towards your dreams, you're doing a fantastic job! I am so proud of you for staying committed and for challenging your enemies every step of the way.

When you make a decision to follow your Why and do whatever is necessary to reach it, you must have faith. You must have faith in yourself and in the process. When you plant a seed, you don't keep digging it up everyday to see if it's still there. Why not? Because you know that if you continually dig up the seed, then it's not going to grow. You have to plant the seed, put the soil on it, and allow nature's seasons to harvest it. Just like nature goes through seasons, your life goes through seasons too.

There's a reason for every season that you go through in life. It's not always easy to understand at the time that you are going through it, but is often revealed in the future. One principle that is constant through every season is sowing and reaping. It's been proven that what ever you sow in life, you will eventually reap. Sowing and reaping will never cease. If you don't believe it, then just take a look back at the bad decisions that you made. What were the results of those bad decisions? In other words, what did you reap from those bad decisions. Flip that around, what have you reaped from your good decisions? You plant a bad seed; you get a bad harvest. You plant a good seed; you get a good harvest. It's really just common sense.

  I talk a lot about sowing seeds of greatness in the lives of others to reap a bountiful harvest. I'm not talking about just donating money to charity or buying presents for kids at Christmas. Those are great things, but you can also sow seeds with your words and your actions. Speak prosperity into the lives of others. I love to hear parents speaking life into their small children. "You are a champion. You can do all things. I am so proud of you." Those are seeds of greatness that those parents are planting in the lives of their children. You can also invest your time in a selfless act like volunteering at a local homeless shelter.

  Now, I'm not going to tell you that you will reap a great harvest immediately after sowing a seed. It's possible, but rarely happens that way. Most of the time, you will go through a rainy season first. The rainy season tends to be the tough times when you just don't know if you can hang on to your dream any longer. It's also the time that you are faced with the hardest and most crucial decisions. When it rains, it pours! However, the rainy season will make you stronger. Think about it. A seed couldn't survive or grow without rain. Similarly, you can't grow without facing those challenges and making those hard decisions.

It's okay to make mistakes. Mistakes don't cancel or stop your harvest. You've got to realize that in the growth process, you will make plenty of mistakes. They're essential for the growth. The important thing is to learn from your mistakes and don't keep making the same ones over and over again. One of my favorite quotes by Dennis Waitley is "Mistakes are painful when they happen, but years later, a collection of mistakes is what is called experience." Just consider a mistake a rainy season, but the sun is shining right in the horizon because you learned from it.

After you sow your seeds and experience the rainy season, it's time to reap your harvest. Just as a farmer is patient during the growth of his crops, you must also be patient while preparing for your harvest. One of my coaching students diligently built his business. He worked long hours and didn't take any shortcuts. He grew to see just how hard it was to run an ethical business in today's world. He was also very active in the youth ministry at church. This guy planted seeds of greatness in every area of his life, and he made it through many rainy seasons when his strength was truly tested. Sadly, he grew impatient waiting on his harvest. He just couldn't understand why his business hadn't skyrocketed yet. His impatience led to him becoming completely miserable and eventually giving up. Instead of preparing for his harvest, he went back to just living a mediocre existence and not expecting anything great to happen.

While waiting on your harvest, you have to have an expectation that it's coming. I have this quote taped to my computer keyboard – "I am expecting a supernatural miracle today." You have to live with a spirit of expectation and constantly prepare for your harvest by speaking daily affirmations. Here are a few of my own affirmations – "I have planted seeds of greatness and my harvest is coming! I see my harvest! I feel my harvest! I expect to receive my harvest today!" You've got to make your affirmations personal to you and what type of harvest that you are expecting. Affirmations are just your faith verbalized. The Bible says "Let us not grow weary while doing good, for in due season we shall reap if we do not lose heart." In other words, don't give up! Your harvest is just around the corner.

Here's another tough question for you. Are you at a point in your life where you know what you want, but you don't know how to get it or what your next step is? That's okay. You don't have to have the whole process mapped out perfectly before you. The first step is the most important step, and that's to make new decisions and stop making excuses. You've made a decision to move forward and pursue your Why in life. Now, the next step is to figure out how you will achieve your ultimate Why in life. However, you can't develop that plan of action until you can actually see yourself achieving your goals and dreams.

You must create a dream wall in your construction zone. Your construction zone is where you build your business. If you're a network marketer, then your construction zone is likely your home office. If you're a realtor, then your construction zone may be a workspace in someone else's office building. If you're a truck driver, then your construction zone is gong to be in your truck. No matter where your construction zone is located, you must have a dream wall. A dream wall is a collection of quotes, pictures, checks, drawings, affirmations or basically anything that motivates you to achieve your Why in life. The walls of my construction zone are filled with reminders of where I'm going in life and the things that I've already accomplished.

One of the most important things that I want you to do is add more pictures to your construction zone. Attend more events and take pictures of yourself at those events with fellow champions and your mentors. If your construction zone is your car, just be very careful where you put the pictures. When my wife, Christie, and I started dating, I stuck our photo in my car near the speedometer. Christie got in the car one day and asked what was burning. I didn't realize that I had placed the photo over the temperature gauge, and I literally blew up my engine. No kidding. I had to trade that car in the next day. So, you see that I am serious about having photos EVERYWHERE!

When you get down and out, just look at your dream board. If you see it, then you can believe it. The world is full of distractions, and it's really hard to stay focused on your dreams. That's why it's so important to plaster reminders all around you. One of my students works in an office setting and is limited on what she can put on her cubicle walls. That didn't stop her! She typed out affirmations and stuck them to her computer. She made a photo collage of her family, goals and dreams and put it in a little frame on her desk. Whenever she feels challenged by her JOB, she just looks at down at those constant reminders about where she is going in life.

You have the right to achieve your Why and your dream board will keep that in perspective for you, but sometimes those little excuses slip back in the crevices of doubt and fear. The excuses begin to cloud your vision like the fog. Every time you make an excuse, it gets a little thicker. Christie and I often drive up to our cabin in the Smoky Mountains, and there's a reason for the area being called "Smoky Mountains." At times, the fog is so thick that you can't see the taillights of the car in front of you. If you don't follow the caution signs, you will smash into another vehicle or run off the side of the road.

It's the same with that cloud of excuses. Your dream vision is blurred and you can barely see your Why in life. At this point, you either take notice of the caution signs and stop the excuses or you will have zero visibility and smash right into adversity. You don't have to get to this point! If you catch yourself making excuses and avoiding decisions, take a step back and apply what you have learned in this teaching. You now understand excuses are being driven by fear and you have the ability to conquer that fear with your belief.

I don't want to conclude this teaching before covering this question. Why do obstacles, enemies, and unforeseen circumstances come your way? There are several reasons why these negative things occur. First off, recognize that when you're pushing yourself towards the next level of success, you will face adversity. One of my great mentors, Todd Mullins, often says that "If you aren't currently in a battle, then you're either coming out of one or preparing for the next one." Adversity is unavoidable on your success journey. If you didn't have to face obstacles in life, then how would you build your strength to conquer the next giant that gets in your way? Allow the adversity to drive you and make you stronger!

One major thing that causes adversity is the junk in your life. The junk I am talking about refers to the people or things holding you back. You can't move to the next level while simultaneously holding onto this junk that's keeping you in your comfort zone. For example, if you attend personal development events on the weekends, but continue to hang out with the same negative friends that don't believe in you, then how can you expect to move forward? Here's another one for you. If your dream is to build a successful business, but the only type of knowledge that enters your eyes and ears is bad television and gossip magazines, how do you expect to promote your belief level so that you can see yourself achieving that dream? It's really not rocket science. You just need to take action and clean the junk out of your life once and for all.

You must begin living your why NOW. Not tomorrow, not next month, not next year. You must begin living your dream NOW! As long as you continue to see your Why as occurring in the future, that's where it will always be—in the future. Start living and acting as though your Why is true right now. Who would you associate with? How would you spend your time? In what ways would your life be different? Start today and create an action plan in order to reach your goals and dreams. What sorts of things do you need to do in order to reach those dreams? Write them down and begin to take action on them. Even if you can only think of two things, write those two things down and take action.

More ideas and opportunities will begin to come your way once you make the decision to take action. As the great Martin Luther King, Jr. said, "You don't always have to see the whole staircase. Just take the first step." Take that first step TODAY by making a decision to commit to your goals and dreams. Once again…Decision plus action equals results. To achieve the results that you desire, make the decision to get committed and take those action steps toward the achievement of your Why.

Follow the words of the great Napoleon Hill, who wrote *Think and Grow Rich*. He said "If you want to be successful, you must stop making excuses and instead make decisions promptly and definitely. Successful people know what they want and stop at nothing until they get it. They step out in faith and claim what they desire to achieve."

Listen to me. You are one decision away from the next phase of your life, and it's the best phase. It's a more prosperous, successful, and rewarding phase that exists. All it takes is a decision to move forward, stop making excuses and conquer your fears. It's all up to you! You have the tools to do it so now just step up to the plate and take a swing. Even if you strike out the first time, in the game of life you have limitless chances to try again.

Principle VII
Success Lies in Your Seed

Every single person on the face of this Earth has a seed of prosperity within them. We're given our seed of prosperity on the most important day of our lives—our birthday. When we are born, we enter the world on equal playing ground. We have the same opportunities as everyone else to prosper. I know some of you are probably saying, "John, I was born poor. How did I have the same opportunities as a rich person?" You must look past the adversity that you were born into and focus on being born into a world of endless possibilities.

It's not the problems that were already there when you were born that really matter. It's just the sheer fact that as a child you were blessed with a clean slate and a tiny little heart that was open to believing anything was possible. Yes, I know things do happen during our developmental years that deter our ability to achieve our dreams. However, no one can take away that seed of prosperity that was planted in your heart by God. When you're faced with a challenge, have you ever felt that little tug in your heart telling you that you can do it? It's that tiny seed that is deep rooted in your heart that keeps reminding you that you were born for greatness.

The problem is that 97% of people don't know this truth and quiet their heart with fear, doubt and procrastination. They actually believe that the remaining 3% of people in this world that have made the decision to be successful are "lucky". As you know, I don't believe in luck. I refuse to believe in luck! I create my own future based upon the vision that I hold inside of me. I am allowing my seed to harvest. In order for my seed to harvest, I need to feed it. I need to water it. I need to take care of it. As soon as I start ignoring my seed, it starts to die. The roots start to wither. I just simply will not allow the unnecessary death of my seed to happen.

    The success process is not incredibly difficult. All it takes is daily focused committed action. That's it! Successful people simply do what unsuccessful people won't do. They immerse themselves in self-development, they build their business, they face obstacles, and they get uncomfortable. More importantly, when they feel the fear rising up, they take that step of faith anyway! They're simply willing to get uncomfortable and fail their way towards success. Am I saying that the process is easy? No. The process is not easy. However, it simply takes daily actions that bring you closer to your goal. Those actions feed and cultivate your success seed.

    The most powerful part of harvest time is the process. The process is when you're cultivating the seed. Cultivating the seed requires time. I'll tell you right now that the fastest way to failure is a shortcut. If you skip essential steps, such as breaking the seed open and expecting to see the fruit, the seed will crumble before your eyes. Instead, gradually take those daily success action steps. Allow your seed to become strong and deepen its roots in your heart.

In the gospel of Mark, Jesus told a story of a farmer that went out to plant some seed. As he scattered the seed across his field, some of the seed fell on a footpath, and the birds came and ate it. Other seed fell on shallow soil with underlying rock. The seed sprouted quickly, because the soil was shallow. But the plant soon wilted under the hot sun, and since it didn't have deep roots, it died. Other seeds fell among thorns that grew up and choked out the tender plants so they produced no grain. Still other seeds fell on fertile soil, and they sprouted, grew, and produced a crop that was thirty, sixty, and even a hundred times as much as had been planted.

What does this parable have to do with your success? Everything! If the seed of prosperity in your heart isn't nurtured, it will die. As you see from the story, the only time the seed flourished was when it was planted in fertile soil. Many times, we try to position ourselves in the places where the world tells us that we belong instead of taking those daily action steps to determine where we are really meant to be in life. Let me ask you a serious question, "Are you surrounded by thorns that are slowly choking your dream?" If so, it's time that you replant your seed in fertile soil. How? I'm going to teach you how to take care of your seed of prosperity by breaking down the word "seed".

The first letter in the word seed is "S", which stands for submerge. Visualize an overflowing chocolate fondue fountain with chocolate gushing out everywhere. You place a marshmallow on a dipping stick and just barely place it in the stream of chocolate. No, that's ridiculous. We all know that you stick that marshmallow in the chocolate until it is fully covered...submerged. I've actually seen little kids stick their whole hand in the fountain just to make sure that they have as much chocolate on their marshmallow as possible.

When it goes to growing your seed, you have to be like that little kid at the fondue fountain who believes that there is no limit to the amount of chocolate that he can receive. You must submerge yourself in personal development on a daily basis to build your belief in yourself and that little seed in your heart. As the success and motivation enters your eyes and ears, the belief nutrients flow through your heart and the roots of the seed deepen and become stronger. You begin to truly see that all your dreams and goals are possible. Poverty and lack are no longer a reality for you in any area of your life. Remember, you were blessed with this seed of prosperity at birth, and it's ready and willing to accept that vital nutrition from the positive messages that you are immersing yourself in daily.

We are surrounded by negativity in the world, and you must clean out all the garbage that you allowed to enter your mind. I call this brainwashing. You wash your physical body to rid it of dirt so why wouldn't you wash your mind of all the negative nonsense that the world tells you? For example, suppose you are building your business but still work at a job to fund your entrepreneurial dream. All day long, your co-workers tell you how impossible it will be for you to build a business in this economy. When you go home and start focusing on your business, you are distracted by those naysayer thoughts still lingering in your head. This is the exact time that you have to wash those thoughts right out of your mind.

How? Watch a motivational DVD, listen to an inspirational CD or read a book about other successful entrepreneurs. Say your affirmations out loud and declare that you will achieve your dream. Focus on the pictures on your dream board of your family and visualize your freedom date. Submerge yourself in personal development. The roots of your seed will grow strong and you will be able to withstand any type of adversity that gets between you and your dream.

The next letter is "E" for explore. Thus far, we've talked about feeding your seed so that it can become stronger, but now I want to explore what lies inside your seed. Let's go back to the day that you were born into this great world and that tiny little seed of prosperity came alive in your heart. As you grew, the seed absorbed whatever you fed it. Imagine a four year old dreaming of being a superhero. He's running around the house with a pillowcase draped around his neck as a cape and his arms stretched out in front of him. There is nothing that you could say to him to make him believe that it isn't possible for him to fly around and save the world from bad people. That child's belief in his dream and the words that he speaks about that dream constantly feed the seed in his heart no matter how unrealistic that dream may seem to everyone else. The seed is sprouting and the roots begin extend deep into the child's heart.

Now, imagine that same child fourteen years later. He's getting ready to go off to college and start his own life or maybe he's taking over the family business. In his mind, he knows that it will be difficult but believes that it is possible. That belief in his dream and encouragement from his support system feeds the seed in his heart. No matter what challenges he has faced thus far, his seed of prosperity is strong and protected by his dedication to his dream and determination to succeed.

Then around the age of twenty-five, it happens. He starts to let others tell him what he's capable of achieving, and he begins to limit himself based on the ideals of society. The seed in his heart starts to wither and is no longer receiving the nutrients from his belief that it needs to survive. Unless he makes the decision to rebuild that belief and refuses to listen to the naysayers, his seed of prosperity will die and the likelihood of him achieving his dreams will diminish.

Is this where you are in your life? Have you allowed the naysayers and adversities that you face to determine your level of success? If so, it's not too late. Right now, your seed may be buried underneath years of fear, procrastination and doubt but you can change that. It's not the end of your dream unless you give up, which leads right into the next letter of the word "seed".

It's another "E", but this time it stands for excavate. There are many definitions of this word but the one that I like the most is "to expose or uncover by digging." If your seed of prosperity is covered up by the rocky soil of fear, doubt, and procrastination, then it's time that you take out your big shovel of faith and start digging. Don't stop until you've uncovered that tiny little seed that is fighting to stay alive. During this process, you have to put an end to all the outside influences in your life controlling your level of success. If you are hanging out with negative friends, STOP! If you are watching trash television shows, STOP! Whatever you are doing or allowing to enter your mind that is burying your seed deeper in that rocky soil STOP!

The final letter in the word seed is "D" for devotion, which is defined as a commitment to some purpose. You must be completely, undeniably devoted to your seed of prosperity. You will do ANYTHING that's legal, moral and ethical to protect your seed…your dream…your Why in life. To develop this type of devotion, you simply take a step back to the first letter in this teaching – "S" for submerge. If you aren't completely submerged in personal development, then it will be easy for the enemy to annihilate your self-belief. No matter how much you want to achieve your dreams, there's no way that your seed of prosperity will flourish if you don't believe in yourself. The only person that can make you give up is YOU!

Of all the battles that a Navy Seal must fight, none is more important than the first – mind over body, and this battle is fought during "Hell Week", which is one of the most grueling times for the trainees. They are constantly cold, hungry, wet, sleep-deprived and continuously moving. Throughout Hell Week, the instructors continually remind candidates that they can "Drop-On-Request" (DOR) any time they feel that they can't go on by simply ringing a shiny brass bell that hangs prominently within the camp for all to see. One instructor actually said "The belief that it's all about physical strength is a common misconception. Actually, it's 90 percent mental and 10 percent physical. Trainees just decide that they are too cold, too sandy, too sore or too wet to go on. It's their minds that give up on them not their bodies."

You have to be as devoted to your dream as the Navy Seal is to conquering Hell Week. Don't let those negative thoughts that have been planted in your mind by naysayers be the reason that you DOR and ring that shiny brass bell that signifies that you gave up on yourself and that little seed of prosperity in your heart. Devote yourself to achieving what some see as unrealistic by immersing yourself in personal self-development. Your devotion will yield results that you've only dreamed of!

So many people aren't willing to devote themselves to their dreams and pay the price for success. I can tell you right now that if you don't pay the price for success, you will fail. Whatsoever you sow, you shall reap. If you sow a failure mentality, that's what you'll get—failure. If you sow a success mentality, that's what you'll get—success. Some people don't agree, but I just tell them to take a good look at their life. It's impossible for them not to see that their life results are a result of their willingness to pay the price.

I've got to forewarn you. The information I'm going to share with you now is not for everyone. Not everyone can handle the truth. The truth is that you must take responsibility for where you are at in your life. If you don't take responsibility for your life, that means you place the blame elsewhere. You blame the weather, the economy, your friends, your relatives, your employer, etc. The list goes on and on, because it's easier for most people to point fingers at someone else for their failure than to say it was their own fault.

As long as you place blame elsewhere, your success will always be determined by those outside factors. You will only be successful when the weather, the economy, your friends, your relatives, and your job are perfect. You will only reach success when all of the outside forces are aligned and everything falls into place on its own. Guess what? That day is never going to come! The longer you delay claiming responsibility for your life, the longer you are delaying your success. You will become a success once you take responsibility for your life and make a decision to change and stretch yourself.

I don't want you to finish this book, stick it on a shelf and forget everything that I've taught you and that you've learned about yourself. To tie all this together and give you a plan of action to start implementing as soon as you finish this book, I'm going to unveil thirteen secrets behind the success seed process that will catapult your life results. I'm going to pull back the curtain and lay out what your future's going to look like once you decide to make a difference. Some people think that thirteen is an unlucky number, and there are even hotels that don't have a thirteenth floor. Of course, there's a thirteenth floor, but they just refuse to call it that because of foolish superstition. I'm shattering the myth about the number thirteen by giving you these thirteen life-changing secrets.

Secret number one is to find the possible. So often, people focus on if something is impossible or why something is possible. It's the "only if" mentality that makes them think that something major has to happen for their dreams to even be a remote possibility. They choose to see the reasons why their success seed cannot be cultivated and grown instead of focusing on the possibilities within their own hearts.

One of the laws of the universe is the law of opposites. This law states that everything must have an opposite, and that without an opposite, something cannot exist. Inside the word impossible is possible. Within every impossibility is a possibility. Both exist simultaneously just as failure and success exist simultaneously. You have both a success seed and a failure seed within you. It's just a matter of which one you choose to focus on and cultivate.

You have to create a legacy for your life. A legacy is defined as a gift of personal property, something handed down from the past. You have to make a decision to stretch out beyond your comfort zone and move beyond all of your excuses. I refuse to accept excuses, either from myself or someone else. I refuse to accept excuses from people who are highly capable of achieving success. How do you know if you're capable of achieving success? If you have a pulse and a birthday, then you are highly capable of achieving success. Start seeing the possible that lies within the impossible, and you will begin to cultivate the success seed process.

Secret number two is that a seed is powerless until it's planted. What happens to the seeds that remain in an unopened package?

Nothing. They could be the most expensive and highest quality seeds available, but unless you open the package and plant them, they will never sprout and grow. They remain lifeless in a paper bag that is preventing them from reaching fertile soil.

The same thing can be said about your dream. Your dream is never going to harvest unless you plant it. You could have the most elaborate, well thought out, highly creative dream ever developed on the face of the Earth. However, if you don't plant your seed in fertile soil and provide the nutrients that it needs to survive, then your seed of prosperity will be trapped inside its own paper bag of fear, doubt and procrastination.

I've seen photos of dream walls of people from all over the world. These walls are made up of pictures and writings that describe that particular person's ultimate dreams in life. Sadly, most of these people will never achieve that level of success that they so desire, because they didn't plant those seeds of hope anywhere other than on that wall. They do nothing else to cultivate the harvest that they've dreamed of for so long. These same people have stood up in my boot camps and passionately read about their Why in life and what they will do to achieve it. Yet, they don't take the next step…action! Remember, if the seed is not planted, then it is powerless. Take the action steps that you've learned in this book, and it's nearly impossible for you not to achieve your dreams.

Secret number three states that your success seed must be in protective and moist ground. You want your seed to be in a healthy and protective environment. Everyone instinctively knows to put seeds in soil and not in between rocks. They know that in order for the seed to grow, they must keep the soil moist by continually watering it. They don't just water it once and walk away expecting it to water itself. They plant it in healthy soil and feed it by keeping it moist.

How do you keep your success seed moist? What sort of thing provides your success seed with moisture? The moist ground for your success seed is your mastermind team. The people that you surround yourself with on a daily basis either moisten or dehydrate your success seed. Do you notice how the importance of your mastermind team keeps appearing over and over again in these different success principles? Your mastermind team literally affects every area of your life as do the negative people in your life.

One of my great friends, Vic Johnson, says, "It is a fool that thinks he or she can run a business in complete isolation." The larger your business gets, the larger your goals get, the more people you will need. Not only will you benefit from having a large mastermind team, but your teammates will benefit from being a part of your team. They're working towards a common goal while achieving their own personal goals. You are planting seeds of greatness in their lives.

The negative people in your life are just as important as your mastermind team. Your negative associations show you how NOT to think, how NOT to feel, and how NOT to treat people. They show you what habits NOT to cultivate, and how NOT to spend your free time. I'm not encouraging you to hang out with these people, but I do want you to learn what NOT to do so that you don't end up with their life results. These people are rocky soil so don't plant your success seeds in that type of environment.

Secret number four for the success seed process is to be incorruptible. When something is incorruptible, it can't be destroyed. It can't rot or decay. Once you plant the seed, it doesn't change. You just need to place it in the right soil with the right people and continually moisten it through your daily actions. Let me give you an example of an incorruptible process of growth. If you plant a tomato seed, water it and protect it from insects, then you will harvest a red, juicy tomato. Growing a tomato requires continuous action. When you cease taking action, the growth process is corrupted.

Similarly with your success seed, you've got to be moving and taking action in order for it to grow and harvest. As long as you're taking daily actions that move that seed towards fruition, that seed is incorruptible. Your enemies and naysayers can try and destroy it, but that seed cannot be destroyed. It's protected from all outside negative influences that could try to kill it and stop you from achieving your dreams.

Secret number five is the realization that your success seed is undeniable. Once your seed becomes incorruptible and nothing stands between you and your dream, your success is undeniable. Your seed is going to sprout, and the fruit is going to ripen. It's inevitable that seed is going to grow! The reason I'm here today as a speaker, coach, and trainer is because I made a decision and paid the price through hard work, perseverance, and dedication to my Why in life. I knew that my success was undeniable, and I created massive action in my life to make my dreams a reality. Your success is undeniable when you take consistent daily action towards achieving your goals and dreams. Start taking action today to create your results for the future.

Secret number six deals with the importance of the seed husk. Let me explain. Every seed has a protective husk. If the husk is removed too early in its growth process, then the seed is vulnerable to things that can kill it. You must develop this same type of protective covering for your success seed especially in the early stages of building your belief system. It's nearly impossible for you to protect that little seed of prosperity in your heart that hasn't even begun to flourish if your belief in yourself and your dreams is not strong enough to withstand the negative storms of life.

Think of a beautiful butterfly that fights to get out of the cocoon that has protected it from danger during its developmental stages. As it struggles to get out of the cocoon, the strength of its wings increases. Have you ever seen a butterfly being blown about aimlessly by a strong breeze? Of course not! The wings are able to withstand the strong force. How are they able to do that? The wings developed their strength during the struggle of the cocoon process.

Just like the seed husk and butterfly cocoon, you must develop a protective covering over your success seed (your dream) until it's ready to be exposed to the world. To create this shield for your dream, you will simply no longer listen to or read garbage that hinders your growth plus you will get away from negative associations that cause you to doubt yourself. As long as your dream stays inside of its cocoon, you don't risk failure. You don't risk ridicule. Yet when you choose to go for your dream and break the cocoon, that's when you develop your strength. That's when you grow and become the person that God created you to be.

Secret number seven is this…the vulture will steal your harvest unless your seed is planted. You have the right to own your seed, because it's YOUR seed. As we've discussed, you've got to plant and protect that seed. Just as a farmer needs to plant and protect his seed in order for it to harvest, you must plant and protect your dream. Otherwise, the vultures, the enemies of your life, will steal it from you.

I talk a lot about the strength of an eagle, and the admiration that I have for these great birds. It's interesting that the vulture and the eagle look a lot alike from a distance yet they have very different habits and habitats. A vulture hangs out on the side of the road looking for dead, smelly, and nasty road kill. They eat the leftovers of rotten animals. An eagle protects its territory and soars above the beautiful canyons. Its food consists of fresh salmon, which makes it stronger not disgusting rotting animal corpses. When a storm comes, the eagle rises above the storm. It gets its strength and energy from the winds generated by the storm. For a vulture, when a storm comes, it goes behind a dirty and disgusting area, waits for something that's about to die, and takes it.

Champion, I want you to ask yourself a question. Who's your vulture that lurks around every corner and tries to steal something that doesn't belong to him like your dream? Is your vulture your belief structure, procrastination, fear or possibly a friend that you know doesn't believe in you. Your vulture is anything that is keeping you from living the life that you desire to live. Make the decision today to stop allowing the vulture(s) in your life to feast on your success seed. Start to soar with eagles and realize that you too have the strength to make it through life's storms. You too are majestic and deserve only the best!

Secret number eight deals with the fact that you are going to shed some blood, sweat and tears to get to where you want to go in life. The process isn't going to be easy. You're going to have to push yourself like you've never pushed yourself before. Just remember that the struggle makes the victory that much sweeter.

Are you willing to put up with the blood, sweat, and tears for your dream? If you're not, then you might as well quit now. Stop wasting your time, because when times get tough, you won't make it. You'll quit at the sign of the first hurdle. If it were easy, then 97% of people would be successful, and only 3% would be broke. Unfortunately, that's not the success statistics of today. People that have been in the success game for a while are starting to give up. They stop associating with other champions. They stop attending events. They stop reading motivational books. They stop watching motivational movies. Instead, they start listening to the naysayers and believing the gloom and doom prophesized daily by the media. These people simply aren't willing to fight for their dream!

Are you willing to put up with the blood, sweat, and tears? My trials and tribulations caused by my stuttering were so rough that some people still simply don't believe it. It's hard for people to grasp the fact that I contemplated suicide, because I was unable to speak like everyone else. I'm here to tell you that I fought the fight of my life to learn how to speak fluently and become a motivational speaker. I shed blood, sweat and tears to get to where I am today. I'm living proof that you can overcome adversity in your life, but you have to be willing to fight and I mean fight hard for your dream.

Be silent, listen closely and you will hear secret number nine. Do you hear it? It's that little seed of prosperity in your heart screaming out for you to take charge of your dream. It knows EXACTLY what you need to do. It knows how to get you from where you are now to where you want to be for the rest of your life. If you listen, you can hear it. What is it saying? It's telling you to take action in order to achieve your dreams and be willing to take risks to cultivate your harvest.

What else is that seed saying to you? It's saying, "Please delete the negative, know-it-all, nasty people from your life." Your success seed knows who those people are. YOU know who they are so why haven't you disassociated with them yet? What's stopping you? Are you afraid of what other people will think? Let me give you a reality check. Those people, whose opinions you're so concerned with, are not your mastermind team. They do not want you to succeed! Chances are they're going to tell you not to even think about it. Listen to your seed and your heart! It's time to move on from your negative associations.

Your seed is also telling you that the harvest is plenty, but the committed, dedicated people are few. The harvest, the success life, is available to everyone. Everyone can become a success. It is entirely possible for 100% of people to be successful and for 0% of people to be failures. We live in an infinitely abundant universe. Opportunities are endless. You can literally be, do, and have whatever you want. People just aren't willing to be dedicated and committed to their dream. The seed in their hearts is screaming, shouting, jumping up and down, and banging its fists. Yet what do 97% of people do? They tell that seed to shut up! They drown it out and stunt its growth forever by refusing to believe that they too can succeed. You must listen to your seed and be willing to do what it takes to achieve your dream.

This brings me to secret number ten, which is to be confident in yourself and your success seed. Know that you deserve to achieve your dreams. The enemy will do all that it can to attack your seed. It will try to cause doubt and confusion. How do you handle such confrontation? Don't argue or become defensive. Refuse to be drawn into controversy. Instead, remain cool, calm, and collected, because you know who you are and what you are capable of achieving.

The enemy often tries to create chaos to distract you from your daily action steps. This chaos often involves gossip and some other form of useless conversation that causes you to waste time and/or lose complete focus on your dream. It also involves some type of activity that throws you off course. For example, let's say that you've been planning on attending a success seminar for months. You have your plane tickets and hotel room. You are pumped and ready to go. When your so-called friend hears about your trip, he starts telling you that it's a waste of money and time. Instead of defending your position, simply don't allow his comments to affect you. He's entitled to his opinion, but it's YOUR life!

Remember, the enemy wants to cause chaos and controversy. Your ultimate defense is serenity and confidence. There's always going to be friction or some type of challenge that hinders your success. However, it's how you deal with it that determines its impact on your level of success.

Secret number eleven in the success seed process is that you will achieve explosive results with daily, laser-focused attention. When you start to pay attention to the seed process, you will start to get paid from your dream process. Just by staying focused, your dream will begin to build upon itself. One of the greatest reasons for failure in life is a lack of focus. There's a baseball coach by the name of Beetle Bailey who understood the vast importance and power of focus. He believed that the key to baseball is pitching, and he had an exercise that he had the players go through. This exercise separated the pro baseball players from the amateurs.

He would give the player a crystal ball. He would say, "When you're ready, throw that ball into the catcher's mitt without his glove having to move. You've got one shot, one tryout, one pitch practice. You know what needs to be done as a pitcher. Get laser focused. If you miss the mitt, you're not playing for me." He knew that he wanted the best baseball team in the world. This seemingly simple exercise helped him to separate the pros from the amateurs. As a result of his laser focused decision to recruit the best, he won eight collegiate World Series championships in a row.

Champion, let me ask you a question. Listen very carefully to what I'm about to say. Are you focused everyday on the success seed process? You've got to get laser focused on which direction you're headed in. Without focus, you'll never truly know where you're going or how you are going to get there. You must focus your attention on the seed process in order to achieve the unimaginable level of success that you desire.

Secret number twelve is incredibly important. It's the basic understanding that the seed process is a minimum of two to five years. This is what really frustrates me to no end. People will say, "John, this motivation stuff doesn't work! I tried it for a year. I tried it for six months. I tried it for a week. It didn't do anything for me!" Champion, you cannot expect immediate results when you embark upon the success journey.

You've been living your life in a certain way for many, many years. It takes time for you to build a new foundation and grow your success seed.

Every goal has a gestation period, and the bigger the goal, the longer the gestation period. I know that when you decide upon something, you want it to manifest right away. It's our normal longing for immediate gratification. But you can't go from where you are to where you want to be in a day, a week, a month, or even a year. The shorter the amount of time required to reach your goal, the smaller the goal must be. Anyone can set and achieve a small goal. It takes a truly successful person to set and achieve a big, hairy, scary, audacious goal.

I didn't achieve my goals overnight. It took me six years to be able to speak fluently. Six years! Do you think that I wanted to be able to speak after only a month's time? Of course! But I knew that I needed to cultivate my success seed. I had to allow it proper harvest time. I remained in my cocoon until I could speak fluently and reach financial freedom. I ultimately overcame my adversity and achieved my Why in life. I encourage you to be patient and remain devoted to your seed of prosperity. Success is inevitable if you follow through with the seed process, but it's not an overnight journey.

Secret number twelve is staying strong during the rainy season. In order for your seed to sprout, it must be watered. It must be fed. The most important part of the growth process is the moisture that comes from the rain. Here in South Florida, we often have water restrictions during the summer months. To prevent the grass from dying, you will see people watering their lawns with jugs of water that they bought from the local market. Why? Because they know that their grass and flowers will die without water.

Without that rainy season, your seed will never grow. It's hard to believe that the rainy season and tough times are beneficial especially when everything seems to be going wrong. When it's raining and the lightning is striking overhead, focus on the rainbow at the end and understand that your level of growth will be so substantial that it will radically change the rest of your life.

Last but not least, secret number thirteen focuses on the words that you speak every day. Every single word that comes out of your mouth is a seed, and those same words determine your future. They tell you where you're going to be a month, a year, five years from now. You own your future by the words you speak. I can tell within thirty seconds of talking to someone which direction their life is headed in.

Successful people speak in a certain way. They decide what they want and go for it. They speak words of prosperity into their lives and believe that the words that flow from their lips will determine their future. I've never heard a billionaire say something is impossible or that he is incapable of achieving a dream. Many times, successful people are thought to be egotistical because they are so confident in their speech and how they carry themselves.

Unsuccessful people also speak in a certain way. They say things like, "I'm sure it's a great business, but nothing ever works out for me. I need to ask my friends first. It's too good to be true." They focus on the impossibility of a situation instead of believing that all things are possible. These people don't understand that life and death lives in the power of the tongue. If they understood this principle, then they definitely would not choose to speak negativity over their lives. They wouldn't cap their success with their words.

If you aren't sure what type of words you speak, ask someone close to you. Ask your mastermind team if you tend to speak words of abundance and possibility, or words of lack and limitation. If you don't have a mastermind team right now, then invest in a small recording, put it in your pocket and press record when you begin your day. You will likely be surprised how your words are shaping your future.

Inside the word challenge is change. Challenge yourself to start speaking new words, to start stretching yourself, and to start expecting differently. Don't be afraid to speak your affirmations out loud. I guarantee that your life will change if you speak prosperity and abundance on a daily basis.

Now that I have shared these thirteen highly guarded secrets with you, it's time for you to take action. Start to plant and cultivate your success seed harvest immediately. The sooner you start, the better! There really is no reason to procrastinate. Don't continue to let fear keep you from moving forward. You deserve so much more than that! I want you to keep the momentum. Keep the motivation. Keep the inspiration. Keep the excitement. Keep the energy. Keep the enthusiasm. Stay focused on your goals. If you do the things that I have been telling you to do, five years from now, people around you will look on in amazement, wishing that they could follow in your footsteps. You can smile knowing that all it takes is a decision and the belief that everything is possible.

Conclusion

Congratulations Champion on finishing this book! Now, I encourage you to go out and live the Champion life that you truly deserve. I would love to hear what you liked best about this book and what new steps you are taking to live the Champion life so email me at John@LifestyleFreedomClub.com.

Notes

Principle I
- Resources relating to the story of Sago Mine and Randy McCloy
    - http://mccloyupdates.blogspot.com/
    - http://en.wikipedia.org/wiki/Sago_Mine_disaster

Principle IV
- Resource for complete story of Sarah Reinertsen
    - http://en.wikipedia.org/wiki/Sarah_Reinertsen
- Resource for complete story of Nancilea Foster
    - http://www.sbcbaptistpress.org/bpnews.asp?id=28688

Principle VI
- Resource for complete story of Jacqueline Saburido
    - http://www.helpjacqui.com/home.htm